Folklore of the
COTSWOLDS

Folklore of the
COTSWOLDS

June Lewis-Jones

TEMPUS

First published 2003, reprinted 2006

Tempus Publishing Limited
The Mill, Brimscombe Port,
Stroud, Gloucestershire, GL5 2QG

British Library Cataloguing in Publication Data.
A catalogue record for this book is available from the British Library.

ISBN 0 7524 2930 2

Typesetting and origination by Tempus Publishing Limited
Printed in Great Britain by Midway Colour Print, Wiltshire

CONTENTS

To my husband, Ralph, and our grandsons
Samuel, Thomas and Christopher

Acknowledgements

I am grateful to the many people who have helped in getting the material for this book. In addition to those who are named in context for answering my many questions, allowing me access to school log books, church records, private diaries and letters, I wish to thank the following: the Archivist and Record Agent at the County Record Office, Gloucester; various Brothers of Prinknash Abbey; staff at the Royalist Hotel and Councillor Mayor Vera Norwood of Stow-on-the-Wold; Jonathan Howard, steward of Snowshill Manor; the curator of Charlbury Museum; West Oxon Arts; the Ghost Research Foundation; Frances Melling for bringing to my attention the Sherborne Mummers Play, and Jack Saunders who recalled it in 1980; Pat Ballinger for details of the Wap Whipot, and Peggy Perrin for memories of old Painswick; Ray Borrett for the background of Bampton Morris Men, and David Quiney for snippets on The Fleece at Bretforton.

I appreciate the generosity of Marjorie Fennessy for allowing me to fillet and filch from the correspondence between her and Dr Russell Wortley on the Morris tradition, and that of Richard Chidlaw for all his interest and generous contribution on folk songs. Thanks, also, to the keeper of the archives at Queen's College, Oxford University; and staff of the National Trust and the Tourist Information Centres in and around the Cotswolds. For various background notes on Tetbury and the Wool Sack Races, I am grateful to Geoff Haines of the History of Tetbury Society, and to Jean Haines for the photograph. To Chris Fothergill of Northleach I am grateful for help on the ancient Charter and to Charles Smart for explaining the role of the Court Leet. Special thanks go to Peter Juggins of Chedworth for sharing his fund of local knowledge, for drawing his recollection of the medieval wall painting, and his work in helping to trace the history of Rose Cottage. In this context, I very much appreciate the assistance given to me by Cathleen R. Latendresse, Manager of Off-site Research Services, Henry Ford Museum, USA, who supplied both historical detail of Rose Cottage and a genealogical tree of the families who had lived in the cottage – all at very short notice. Likewise, for the potted history of the Shakespeare birthday celebrations and her interest, I am grateful to Liz Flower, secretary of the Shakespeare Birthday Celebrations Committee.

I would like to mark my appreciation – and admiration – for photographers of the past, whom I have been unable to contact, for their atmospheric pictures, of which I have reproduced a handful from sixty-year-old issues of *Gloucestershire Countryside*. In particular I wish to mention H.H. Albino and Amy M. Walters, but also anyone else whose pictures I have used. Many have come into my possession over the years and in most cases the sources are quite unknown to me. Other photographic credits are due to Jean Haines (Tetbury Wool Sack Race), and Peter Juggins (Bandsmen of Chedworth and Rose Cottage both in Chedworth and in the USA).

I am also grateful to my friends Jim and Barbara Mason for directing me to John O'Keefe of The Sherborne Arms, whose help and interest in getting details of the old Burford and Bibury races are much appreciated; to Mrs Strange of Ducklington for patiently answering my questions on the village's Fritillary Sunday; Barbara Radcliffe, manager of the Oxfordshire Cotswolds Visitor Information Centre, and Skip Walker, editor of the *Stroud News and Journal* – a big thank you.

Last, but by no means least, my sincere thanks to David Buxton of Tempus Publishing for his patience and interest in getting this book into print – and to my husband, Ralph, for his steadfast support and encouragement.

June Lewis-Jones
Spring 2003

INTRODUCTION

The definition of folklore in the Concise Oxford Dictionary is given as 'the traditional beliefs and customs of the people'. The definition of the Cotswolds is somewhat more open to interpretation: the pedantic will opt for the geographical area based on geological foundations of the oolitic limestone from the sharply-defined escarpment on the western edge tilting by way of hills and wolds to the Windrush Valley, edging into Oxfordshire on the eastern side, and north to south from Chipping Campden to Bath. But a region cannot be defined as sharply as an administrative county boundary drawn on a planner's map. The Cotswolds are visibly identifiable by their tangible characteristics, such as the distinctive architectural style of buildings and boundary walls of native stone, but the character belongs to the folk of the Cotswolds, and it is the lore, language and legend making up their beliefs and customs which give them that identity, rooted in hoary tradition from an ancient past.

The people of today are interested in, and fascinated by, the folklore of their region with arguably more enthusiasm than their forbears; this can be gauged by the number of revivals of old customs that had lapsed for one reason or another over the years and the embryonic beginnings of activities and events which are being established in communities across

Shep Bond with Cotswold sheep of the Garne flock at Aldsworth.

the Cotswolds and will, eventually, become traditions in their own right. After all, every one of our customs and festivals had to start somewhere at some time.

The salvation of folklore perhaps stems from people recognizing it as an integral part of our heritage, not just a slice of social history. We owe it to writers and researchers and chroniclers of the not-so-distant past to preserve for future generations valuable contemporary material on which to build a living tradition.

It is interesting, and provides some degree of parochial pride, that the great Cecil Sharp first encountered folk music – which was to become his life's work, and the recording of it his lasting memorial – on a 'memorable Boxing Day morning in 1899' when he saw the morris dancers at Headington Quarry near Oxford, who were dancing 'out of season to earn extra money to tide them over a hard winter'. They were part of the Cotswold tradition of morris men, and Cecil Sharp was to later make the Cotswolds the major hunting ground for his internationally famous collection of folk songs and dances from which he founded the English Folk Dance Society in 1911. It was folk song that first caught his attention and he scoured the fields and cottages, the almshouses and the workhouses, and stopped on the roadside seeking out the folk who sang these old songs and the tunes to which they fitted the often locally composed words. This was all a far cry from Cecil Sharp's professional work as Principal of Hampstead Conservatoire of Music and music tutor to the children of the royal family. Ralph Vaughan Williams was also to capture the rural and rustic elements, the scriptural simplicity and beauty of country life in a number of his compositions, and today Johnny Coppin produces distinctive Cotswold folk songs and also provides music for other local ballad writers, carrying on the long musical tradition.

At the end of the nineteenth century J. Arthur Gibbs felt the urgency of recording life in his Cotswold village, voicing his concern that the characters and characteristics which he had learned to love and respect we would 'never see the likes of again'. He was particularly fascinated by the dialect of the locals, and odd words and phrases of speech that he wanted the old gamekeeper to interpret for him are to be found jotted down in indelible pencil between disjointed ideas in the small black leather notebooks from which his never-out-of-print classic *A Cotswold Village* evolved. A more academic study of dialects was made by the School of English at the University of Leeds. From the (now defunct) Institute of Dialect and Folk Life Studies, there have been surveys, a dictionary, a book of grammar and a *Linguistic Atlas* to name but a few of the publications using the university's surveys of regional speech. This is in itself some measure of the interest generated in what we say and how we say it. Little did I realise when I started my own collection of words that I had grown up with, and discovered that many of my students at the time did not know what they meant – let alone used them – that it could be of some historic interest one day; that is why I was delighted that my publisher encouraged me to include them in this book. Likewise with some of the dishes and festive fare that are so much a part of our tradition.

Every region has its own folklore, of course, but that of the Cotswolds is particularly rich in its traditions, its legends and wondrous stories that have come down to us through the ages. Their survival is due in no small part to the very localised, truly parochial life of the villagers in particular, until the social changes wrought by two world wars, with people having to move from the country into towns for employment and rapid development of travel widening horizons and experiences. I recall this being illustrated by Laurie Lee, in a treasured memory of when my husband and I met him for a drink in his home local at Slad. 'I did not see Tetbury until I was seventeen,' he said, 'and I thought Tewkesbury was somewhere in Poland. But at nineteen I waved farewell to this valley to see the world. But like the homing birds which return year after year from their wintering in warmer climates, I have returned. Nowhere in the world have I seen anything to replace this special place.'

What a poetic way to say 'it is all about having roots'. And this is what folklore is all about – the beliefs of my childhood, my treasured tales of once-upon-a-time, all intermingled with everyone else's whose roots are firmly in the Cotswolds – and the joy of sharing in the continuity of our sometimes quaint and curious culture which is the lore of the folk.

I

DIALECT

Cotswold folk were well versed in the Scriptures from an early age and related favoured stories in their own tongue – such as this little tale of corn of Egypt which I found in an old (undated) journal cutting tucked between the pages of my grandfather's Family Bible. Many of these words peculiar to the district are still in use today.

Josef was a bit of a dabster of a carn merchunt. Well, a-did kip the kay o' of the carn krib yur in, yur out, til uh was chock vull, an' tha' thur carn enver didn't go fousty. 'Twas a licker as 'ow twas, but tha's ow twas. Any roads on, ee never mooched vrom 'is bisness, an' carn trade weren't never zlack. For severn yur a-scrobbled along ater carn and then fur 'nother seven yur, wot wi' the dumbledores an' the weather all casualty like, thur won't no crops to 'arvest. So ol' Josef got out 'is carn weout badgerin, an' let the peepul of Egipt hev carn to grind in thur housen an' fur thur cattle. No doubt zum on um looked a bit glouty like as thay 'ad to pay a bit steepish for't not 'aving a lug of ground bringin' um a 'andful, but the aith yur was zich a jorum thur were enow for em all.

The Cotswold idiom is fast dying out with changing communities bringing in their varied regional accents and expressions, and the media introducing modernised catch phrases and 'buzz' words, so perhaps it is timely to record those words and sayings once so peculiar to this area, before they are lost forever. Local language is a living culture – dialect is spoken, rarely written, so recording oral history in print has to rely very largely on phonetic spelling.

Dabster	'dab hand', expert
Fousty	mouldy
Scrobbled	worked hard
Dumbledores	bumblebees and cockchafers
Casualty (casual)	inclement (when said of the weather)
Glouty	surly, sulky
Lug	an old English measure of land (15-20ft)
Aith	other (or in this context, the succeeding)
A jorum	a lot, usually applied to quantity of food

Many of the words have survived a thousand years of usage in these parts; many field names are straight from the Saxon farms hereabouts and ancient charters and terriers name fields as grounds. In the same way, older folk stick to the Saxon termination of 'housen' for houses and 'primrosen' for primroses.

J. Arthur Gibbs, the first author to write a classic on the Cotswolds, was obviously intrigued by the dialect spoken in his day in the Coln Valley and warned in his evergreen book *A Cotswold Village*, published in 1898, that 'in twenty years' time it will be a thing of the past'. Gibbs sums up what he learnt of the characteristics of the dialect from 'a great exponent of the language of the country' in these verses:

If thee true Glarcestershire would know
I'll tell thee how us always zays un;
Put I for me, and 'a' for 'o'
On every possible occasion.

When in doubt squeeze in a 'w'
Stwuns, not stones, and don't forget, zur,
That thee must stand for thou and you
Her for she and vice versa

Put 'v' for 'f'; for 's' put 'z';
'Th' and 't' we change to 'd',
So dry an' kip this in thine yead,
An' thou wills't talk as plain as we.

In the mid-sixteenth century, John Smyth wrote in his *Berkeley Manuscripts*:

> There are frequently used certaine words, proverbs and phrases of speech, which wee hundreders conceive to bee not only native but confined to the soile bounds and territory thereof; which if found in the mouthes of any forraigners, wee deeme them as leapt over our wall, or as strayed from their proper pasture and dwellinge place: And doubtless, in the handsome mouthinge of them, the dialect seemes borne of our owne bodies.

The most ancient record now extant of Cotswold dialect in written form appears to be in *The Chronicle of Robert of Gloucester*, a versifying historian who, according to his own statement, lived at the time of the Battle of Evesham, 4 August 1265. It is a language defying definition and, like most of our English speech, carries echoes of the many tongues of those who came to our shores. Of all the invaders who settled, it is the Saxons who had the major influence. Considerably more than just the farming folk they are usually portrayed to be, they were great administrators and it is from them we have our shires parcelling up the ancient kingdoms into identifiable regions, each with its own culture. Many of our field names are pure Saxon and words that have been voiced over a thousand years still give the colour and cadence to the native Cotsaller's speech today.

I coin the term 'Cotsaller' purposefully, to keep faith with Shakespeare's 'Cotsall' for Cotswold. The great bard was well versed in all things Cotswold, his dialogue is punctuated with dialect words, phrases and the home-spun proverbs with which we have all grown up. His use of the double negative crops up again and again; as illustrated by Shylock in *The Merchant of Venice*, act IV: 'so can I give no reason nor I will not'.

Some words rely entirely on context, as can be seen in the glossary of Cotswolds terminology, to be found on pages 203-217, and the expressions, like fine regional wines, are savoured best in the locality in which they were produced and matured.

'A' (pronounced like a soft 'ughh') is frequently used instead of the gender-specific 'he' or 'she', so we have: 'A-axed I avore I 'ad a chance to reckon it out proper, then a-arged the point; a-babbled 'bout the afterclaps till me yud was all a-addled; I can't away with such as they.' 'A' in this case can be male or female and the plural 'they' at the end indicates 'those sort of people' despite talking about one person in this instance.

'Her' is commonly used instead of 'she' but many inanimate objects are masculine, hardly ever 'it'; the feminine is reserved for the mother country and a tom cat – that is a 'she'!

Couplets, rhymes and jingles give the colour and cadence to the Cotsaller's speech: 'Alike an April shower, that wets the stone nine times in an hour' describes a fickle man as changeable as April weather.

> *Athrup, Suthrup and Buthrup*
> *All begins with A*

This little couplet from my corner of the Cotswolds is one of those age-old tricks intending to fool the listener into thinking we are talking about the place names – Hatherop, Southrop and Bouthrop – instead of the word 'all'.

Talk of the Tiler, or the Slatter's Sizing

Cotswold stone roof tiles are often referred to as 'slats', despite the fact that they are not slates in the accepted term. Quarrying for roofing stone was traditionally carried out in the autumn, and the stone was then covered with turf sods to keep it 'green' until the first frosts arrived. The great stone slabs were then uncovered and laid flat on the ground to exclude the air. The 'bed' of the tile expanded by frost made splitting between the layers (the 'pendles') easier. The edges of the tiles were then roughly squared off and a hole pierced centrally at the top for it to hang on a peg on the roof rafters. Stacking the tiles, ensuring they supported each other without collapsing and smashing, was a skilful job. Next they were graded by size in quantities peculiar to the trade: 6 to 18in-long tiles were stacked to 400 (this added up to 100 units) and four piles of twenty-five 19 to 30in tiles (each of these piles also making 100 units) were stacked at the ends; this made 500 units, sufficient to roof ten square feet. A reversal of the baker's dozen, the larger tiles counted as twenty-five to the hundred.

'Slatters' from different areas of the Cotswold had their own jealously guarded names for the tile sizes which were measured on a *wippet stick* marked in Roman numerals – the straight lines being easier to cut than rounded Arabic figures. The following names are listed in increasing order of size, from the smallest at the ridge to the largest over the eaves.

> *Stow on the Wold*
> Short cocks, long cocks, short cuttings, long cuttings, movities,
> short becks, mid-becks, long becks, short bachelors, long bachelors.
> short nines, long nines, short vibbots, long vibbots, short elevens,
> long elevens, short twelves, long twelves (increasing by shorts and
> longs to seventeens).

*Cotswold stone country:
splitting the 'pendles',
c. 1930.*

*Measuring the tiles by a
wippet stick.*

Roof tiles stacked in sizes – note the peg hole in the top.

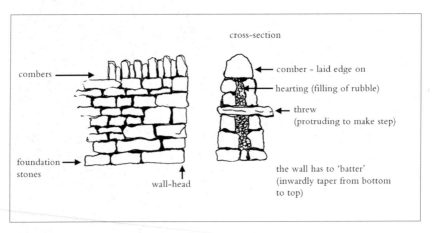

Construction of a Cotswold 'dry-stone' wall.

Bourton-on-the-Water
Short cocks, middle cocks, long cocks, short cuttings, long cuttings, maverday, short backs, middle backs, long backs, short bachelors, short nines, long nines, short wivetts, short elevens, long elevens, short twelves, long twelves, short thirteens, long thirteens (increasing by shorts and longs to sixteens).

Tetbury

Farewells, wippets, chivelers, long chivelers, guardians, long
guardians, cuttings, long cuttings, wivets, long wivets, spots, long
spots, nines, long nines, short tens, long tens (increasing by shorts
and longs to seventeens).

A Shepherd's Calling

Sheep were counted by the score, just as all good country chickens still
lay eggs in dozens, not tens! The old Cotswold shepherds' language was
closely related to the ancient Celtic form:

Yan	one
Tyan	two
Tethera	three
Methera	four
Pimp	five

Counting sheep was always done in twenties.

Remnants of old shepherds' cots found near Miserden.

Sethera	six
Pethera	seven
Hovera	eight
Dovera	nine
Dick	ten
Yan-a-dick	eleven
Tyan-a-dick	twelve
Tethera-a-dick	thirteen
Methera-a-dick	fourteen
Bumfit	fifteen
Yan-a-bumfit	sixteen
Tyan-a-bumfit	seventeen
Tethera-a-bumfit	eighteen
Methera-a-bumfit	nineteen
Gigot	twenty

A stone was dropped on the ground, or put in the pocket as each twenty was reached, then counting started again. The total was calculated by multiplying the number of stones by twenty.

Keeping tally

H. Watkins, a schoolboy reporting for the *Gloucestershire Countryside*, gave an account of a hedger and ditcher working on the piecework system on his father's farm as late as 1940. Unable to read or write, they were using a tally stick:

> He called this keeping tally. After trimming or laying a hedge we would take a piece of string 22 yards in length, and after fastening it to the hedge where he started work, would proceed down the hedge until he reached the end of the string. Then he would cut a stick from the hedge and cut one notch in it. When he had measured the whole hedge, the notches on the stick corresponded with the number of chains he had worked, and we never found an error in his measurements.

There was a medieval practice that involved a more elaborate form of keeping tally on a stick using the same principle. It is believed that one of the reasons why the old Houses of Parliament took fire so quickly, and were so thoroughly gutted, was that the cellars were full of these wooden tallies.

Strength in the weakness

> *Gloucestershire born and Gloucestershire bred*
> *Strong in the arm and weak in the head*

So goes the old ditty, and plenty of honest-to-goodness Glo'shire folk will admit 'I byent no scholard', but it is one of the occasions when the use of the double negative is purposeful, as is the adoption of another consonant to end the word in a sense of determination. A Gloucestershire ploughman is credited with refusing to send his son to school in the 1890s on the grounds that he was taught to spell 'taters' with a 'p'.

One country lad's disdain of a contemporary who was 'learning to be a scholard' was summed up in his remark, 'Thee hast bin to thuck thur school and lurn'd all thick thur jommetry and yet thou cassn't jump thuck thur stowl'.

Here, 'thuck' means that; 'thick' this; 'jommetry' (in this sense) studies; and 'stowl' tree stump. 'Thee' is no doubt a relic of our language's Saxon ancestry used for persons of equal standing; 'thou' was never used to a superior; in this case it was essential to retain 'thee' otherwise it would acknowledge the young learned gentleman's superiority. The exception to this would be in the terminology of the Common Prayer and hymnal when 'Thee' and 'Thou' were respected forms in the traditional sense and never questioned.

Gloucestershire Miles be Long 'Uns

From my magpie collection of tales and sayings, gathered and garnered over the years from sources long lost and forgotten, these are my favourites.

'How far is it to Ciren, my good man?' enquired a traveller of a well-known rabbler [road-scraper].

'Ziren, Ziren?', the old man scrat [scratched] his yud [head].

'Cirencester.'

'Well, dall my rags, thee's be a-meaning Cizziter,' corrected the old roadman. He had been told once by one of them 'long-headed' folk that if they read Shakespeare they'd know that Cirencester was called Cissiter. Not as he'd read Shakespeare, but he reckoned 'twould be a mighty fine book to read, he'd have to find out who wrote it. But that ud 'ave to bide a while, thick yur gent was anxious to get on his way. A right mizzling day it were, too, with the sky a-looking all lowery.

'Well, sir, in this yur sort of hocksey weather 'tis about vour mile, but if thee's a cum yesterday, you'd a got thur in three.'

'Three yesterday but four miles today,' the traveller exploded.

'Well, as I zays, zur, 'tis nation dirty today, a wet day with no rain as thee might zay, but yesterday 'twas the finest day in the parish; roads were dry, three miles with no trouble. Today, so casual like, thee 'as to allow for slippin back a bit.

The traveller spurred on his horse without another word. 'A real funny ossity,' the old rabbler thought as he made his way 'whoam'.

A Tewkesbury Dialogue

A Cotswold variation of where are you going to and can I come too?

> *Wer beest agwoin?*
> *To th' Mythe Tut.*
> *Shall I coom along?*
> *Ay, if thee 'oot.*

Passing thoughts!

On dying – on time or before time!

When a man's owld and a-weered out and begins to get summat the matter wi'ee an' a-do drop off quiet like in 'is bed, 'taint so much to get moithered about. But when a man's 'earty and well an' a-goes 'way from whoam, an a's djed when a-cums back, then 'taint natral-like and a girt sorrow for all o'n um.

'Djed ship,' I zays, 'er yaint a djed ship. Er jest bin killed.'

'Killed un, 'ave 'ee,' er zed; 'dust thee think I cassn't zee that ship wur djed afore thee killed un!'

They says summat every time they d'speak

The Cotswold speech is riddled with simile, e.g. 'as deep as a church'; nothing is simply short or tall, fat or thin. Epigrams from the area often contain a paradox, giving it additional point and vigour:

Up a depth
Not backward in coming forward
It should be there 'cos I can see it
If I was going thur (to a distant place) I 'oodn't start from yur (here)
He 'oodn't be said (wouldn't listen)

Along with the similes, euphemisms also abound:

Sky pilots	vicars
Bible punchers	lay preachers
God botherers	chapel folk
Outriders	travellers for a shop
Counter jumpers	male shop assistants
Calico tearers	female shop assistants

The following Cotswold sayings demonstrate a number of the above characteristics:

Couldn't stop a pig in an alley	a bow-legged person
Would pinch the church if he could get his arms round it	a light-fingered man
He had a good hiding when he was young for giving something away	a mean person
He'd skin a farthing	a miser
As old as a man and a lad	elderly
Like a pig with one ear	lop-sided
He had his teeth curled and his ears pinned further back	smartened up

Under petticoat government	a hen-pecked husband
One eye up the chimney the other in the pot	a cross-eyed person
His brains are where his feet ought to be	mindless person
When his hat's on, his house is thatched	a bachelor
Did a moonlight flit	disappeared
Couldn't cook a man's shaving water	a poor cook
Only four foot and a tater	a short person
No better than she should be	a woman of dubious character
As happy as a cat in a tripe shop	contented
On the glad and sorry	hire purchase (glad to have it and sorry to have to pay for it)
Just with myself	alone

As straight as a yard of pump water
As soft as a ha'poth of soap after a hard day's washing
Poor as a church mouse
Rough and ready like a rat catcher's dog
As hard as the Devil's nutting bag
As black as Herod's heart

My favourite piece was a church notice that my mother used to recite to me – she maintained that it was exactly as the vicar had announced at the end of a Sunday service at South Cerney when she was a girl:

Notices for next Sunday:
The psalm will be one hundred and onety-one.
There will be a meeting on Wednesday to discuss what colour the church
　　will be white-washed.
And the vicar will be nailed to the doorpost.

2

WHAT'S IN A NAME?

The Cotswolds abound with fascinating names. Those of the market towns, villages and hamlets generally comprise their ancient pedigree of noble owners as the first part attached to the 'burg' or 'burgh' (boroughs or manors). By Saxon times this became 'bury', supporting the origins of such places as Tetbury, where it is suggested rather than proven that the name relates to an Abbess Tetta – therefore Tetta's Burg.

The suffix 'ham' or 'ton' (tun), meaning homestead or farm settlement, also relates to the root origin of ownership or position, and sometimes both are used, such as in Meysey Hampton. No trace of the pool from which neighbouring Poulton got its name can now be found, thanks to modern drainage systems. 'Chipping' prefixes (as in Chipping Campden and Chipping Norton) identify the town's importance as a market centre.

Water, the lifeblood of existence, was obviously the deciding factor in settling early communities and therefore features largely in many names. Cardinal points along a river are the easiest to identify, such as Northleach and Eastleach – standing north and east respectively on the River Leach; likewise, North Cerney and South Cerney – but in this case the river, the Churn, is not so readily recognisable due to dialectal

'A Peep in Maiseyhampton', now spelt as Meysey Hampton.

changes in our speech, in the same way as the Ampneys (the 'p' is silent): Ampney St Peter, Ampney St Mary, Ampney Crucis and Down Ampney are linked by the ancient Omenie brook. Lechlade, now promoted for being the highest navigable point on Britain's most famous river has adopted the relatively new title of Lechlade-on-Thames upon whose trade it has grown up, rather than the by now almost streamlike River Leach (Lech) upon which it is laid (lade).

Twin, triplet and quadruplet villages again show their parental ties, each with the other, either by geographical position or size: the Barringtons, Great and Little; the Slaughters, Upper and Lower; the Swells, Upper, Lower and Nether (lower than Lower); the Rissingtons, Great, Little and Wyck (smaller than Little); the Duntisbournes, Abbots, Rouse, Middle and Leer – the latter being hamlets of Abbots; the Badmintons, Great and Little; the Hidcotes, Bartrim and Boyce; the Sodburys, Chipping, Old and Little; and Lypiatt with its Upper, Middle and Nether.

Topographical features were aptly given to such places as Bourton-on-the-Water and Bourton-on-the-Hill, Wotton-under-Edge and Weston-sub-Edge, Snowshill, and the 'combes' – Winchcombe, Pitchcombe and Rendcomb – from 'cumb', meaning valley. The Shiptons: Oliffe, Moyne, Sollars and under-Wychwood, owe nothing to any nautical root and everything to our ancestors' pronunciation of 'sheep'! In the same way, the native stone became the feature from which the 'stan' of Stanway and Stanton evolved, both perfect examples

Stone clapper bridge, linking what were two separate parishes, Eastleach Turville and Eastleach Martin, across the River Leach. The village is now simply called Eastleach.

Shipton-under-Wychwood, the 'sheep-tun' under the ancient forest of Wychwood.

Castle Combe – a picturesque 'combe' village.

Stanton takes its name from the 'stan' (stone) from which it is built.

of how it was used to create the finest buildings in the Cotswold vernacular.

Stonesfield is thought to have been so named as the place where the technique was developed of splitting blocks of limestone into thinner sheets for roofing. Stacked in clamps, similar to how root vegetables were stored, the 'quarry sap' of freshly dug stone was preserved in the clay layers in the oolite. When exposed to frost, the water content of the clay would turn to ice which, when expanded, would split the rock, causing it to foliate like the leaves of a book. It is said that so important was the catching of the first frosts of winter for this stage that the church bell was rung to call the 'slat quarrymen' to the stone fields to uncover the stacked stone for Mother Nature to work her will, thus aiding the production of this natural material. Many of the old 'slatters' referred to all Cotswold roofing stone as Stonesfield slates, although it is not slate in the true sense and a more appropriate term would be 'tilestone'.

Fords, wells and springs have also contributed to the names of a number of places sited thereupon or nearby, including Burford, Fairford, Kempsford, Fulford and simply Ford. Seven Springs, of which there are a number, is used only in the Coberley parish as a specific place name. Westwell takes its name from the nearby well or spring, in the western part of Oxfordshire. The well is not an instantly visible feature of this delightful small village near Burford, however. It is the reed-fringed duck pond that holds centre stage, with the magnificent megalithic monument standing sentinel close by. It is only when you climb up the slope to the small Norman church that you can look down on the water feeding the village pond. Early clues indicate that a Saxon chapel was probably built close to the spring, and the discovery of a huge rough-hewn altar top found under the chancel floor, now returned to its proper place, along with traces of consecration crosses and a Saxon mass dial, add their own historical evidence. In the Middle Ages the Norman lords de Hastings bestowed the advowson on the Knights Hospitaller, who had an important preceptory at Quenington. The Order of Knights had the benefit of several manorial livings in the Cotswolds, but only one perpetuates their endowment in its name: Temple Guiting, one of the two Guitings on the Domesday version of the *Getinge* tributary stream of the upper Windrush. The 'Temple' part of the name identifies it as a holding of the Knights Templar.

The impact of the long-term Roman occupation is seen in the strategic port entrance to the region at *Glevum*, 'the bright place'; it was the administrative Saxons who added the *ceaster*, meaning Roman fort, to give us the present-day shire city of Gloucester. In the same way, Roman *Corinium*, the second largest city in Roman Britain, gained its *ceaster* part of what is today Cirencester. Only a few local people refer to it in Shakespeare's form of Cicester.

Folklorists look to legends for the naming of Oxford and Evesham. Cotswold stone, mainly from the famous Taynton quarries, was transported by the waterways for many of Oxford's most outstanding buildings. The 'city of dreaming spires' in the soft Thames Valley meadowlands was named, so legend has it, as the exact centre of the realm under Lud, son of Beli the Great, King of all southern England some two millennia ago. The story goes that he set his administrators the task of measuring the land from north to south and east to west to pinpoint the axis of his kingdom, and they pinpointed Oxford. As it turned out it proved a fortuitous spot, strategically sited for both road and river crossing, as recorded in the *Anglo-Saxon Chronicle* when Edward the Elder used the town as a buffer against the invading Danes to protect his Wessex lands. It was the capital city for the fugitive monarch in the Civil War and, uncomfortably closer to our own time, it was rumoured that Hitler had chosen Oxford as the centre from which he proposed to govern Britain!

The striking war memorial at Westwell is a memorable feature close by the village duckpond.

Evesham, on the Avon, takes its name from a legendary vision.

Evesham, lying in the fruit vale foothold of the north Cotswolds, owes its name to a much more fanciful – or prosaic, depending on which way you look at it – legend. The old town, surrounded on three sides by the River Avon, was named after a common swineherd called Eoves, who swore that a vision of the Madonna appeared before him at that place. He 'raced' to Worcester (as fast as conditions in AD 701 allowed!) to report this heavenly visitation to the Bishop – who was mightily impressed that this holy beauty 'in raiment infinitely surpassing lilies in whiteness and roses in colour' should grace that place, and ordered that a monastery should be built there forthwith. It was. And what is more, the Bishop decreed that the lowly swineherd should be accorded his rightful due and named the place Eoves' ham. Evesham retains the tower of its old abbey and among its impressive roll of honourable Lords of the Manor was King Canute.

Aston Blank or Cold

Labouring under two names for some four and a half centuries, by 1972 the parish of Aston had had enough, and the council decided to end the confusion with the stroke of a pen: Cold Aston it would be, reverting to

Left: *Aston Blank and Cold Aston are one and the same village.*

Below left: *The church sticks to 'Cold'.*

Below right: *A tombstone in the churchyard says 'Blank'.*

its older name; it was decreed that Aston Blank would exist no longer. But three decades on, those seeking the little upland village beyond tourist-packed Bourton-on-the-Water are still faced with the enigmatic signpost bearing both names – Aston Blank or Cold Aston.

The down-to-earth Saxons first chronicled the lands here as *Eastune,* according to a document in which the King of Mercia gave a portion to the King of Hwiccia – a quite straightforward nomenclature, as the settlement was the easternmost *tun* of the Saxon hundred. The Normans recorded the village at Domesday simply as *Estone* – which became Aston. It was dubbed 'cold' when the Bishop of Worcester inducted a priest to Aston *Frigida* (it is one of the highest of the Cotswold villages at 700 feet above sea level). The church, dedicated to St Andrew, has a Norman nave and chancel and is one of only five churches in the Cotswolds to have no east window. This unusual feature can be traced back to the Celtic missionaries who sheltered only their altars, with the worshippers assembled close by in the open. Shelter for the converts would have been built later to join up with that of the priest and a building developed that was easily defended with limited access.

Aston remained *Frigida* for three hundred years, until a Patent Roll announced the appointment of a vicar to Aston *Blanc*. Previously, the incumbent had been appointed by the priors of Malvern. After the Dissolution of the Monasteries the right of presentation passed to the Crown and this mention was the first presentation for the village by that office. Could it have been in the Lord Chancellor's office that the alias crept in? Perhaps one scribe could not decipher the writing of another and left a blank for the *Frigida* – if it was dictated it would be feasible that it was then written as *Blank*!

Perhaps we shall never know; no family of Blanc, Blank, White or Bare (or any other synonym) has been recorded to account for the change, although it did take the affix of Longechampe for a couple of centuries in acknowledgement of its tenure by that family in the Middle Ages. However, Aston Blank it still remains in the official corridors of county and rural councils, the Inland Revenue and the Ordnance Survey, whereas the parish council, the post office and the locals prefer their Aston Cold to Blank.

As We Know It

Nicknames have been dubbed by locals upon various places throughout history; mainly these would spring from some characteristic of the topography or reputation of the inhabitants, justified or invented by inter-village rivalry or harmless ribaldry, the origins of which have often been lost or distorted very long ago:

> *Mincing Hampton, Painswick Proud*
> *Beggarly Bisley, Strutting Stroud*

Local fare also comes in for mockery:

> *Nympsfield is a pretty place, set upon a tump*
> *But all the folks that live there, eat ag pag dump*

Dursley 'baboons' came in for an even more derogatory reputation, for 'yetting (eating) their pap wi'out any spoons'. If 'pap' suggested a kind of porridge then a very messy picture was painted of the folk of Dursley, who already suffered slights on their integrity and inherent meanness. To be a 'Man of Dursley' springs from the once dishonest practice of some clothiers packing their cloth with 'stuff' to add to its weight. A 'Dursley Lantern' was the tag given to the husbands in pre-street lighting days who, to save the cost of buying a lantern, would lead their wives along in the dark streets by having them cling to their white shirt tails, pulled out to show below the jacket.

'Stow-on-the-Wold, where the wind blows cold' is a fair description for the old town set high on the north wolds, but the additional line of the couplet, indicating it as the place where the cooks have nothing to cook, defies both justification and origin.

Names have been corrupted through derision or dialectal change over the years, such as Yubberton for Ebrington, and much fun has been poked at the Yubberton Yawnies who, it is said, grew their hedges tall to keep the cuckoo in, as they wanted it to be always summertime. Some versifying wag told the tale of:

> *Master Keyte, a man of great power*
> *Lent them a cart to muck the tower*
> *And when the muck began to sink*
> *They swore the tower had grown an inch.*

Master Keyte obviously used his 'great power' to the benefit of more than the 'Yawnies', who manured their church tower to make it grow to the height of the fine one at Chipping Campden, as he founded the Cow Charity in 1632 providing 'the Milk of Ten Good Milch Kine to be distributed from the Tenth of May to the First of November in Perpetuity...' with touching faith in the eternal production of the

There is nothing 'yawnie' about these bright youngsters at Ebrington (Yubberton) in 1989.

humble cow – however, in keeping with the principle of the bequest, the charity still exists in monetary kind.

Shakespeare himself was not above gently ribbing his neighbouring villages, if this doggerel famously attributed to his authorship was true in his day:

> *Piping Pebworth, Dancing Marston,*
> *Haunted Hillborough, Hungry Grafton,*
> *Dodging Exhall, Papist Wixford,*
> *Beggarly Broom, and Drunken Bidford*

Whether by association, or as an attempt to unravel the meaning of the labels attached to the villages, legend has it that it was at the (long-since vanished) Old Falcon at Bidford that Shakespeare and 'the men of Stratford' were 'outdrunk' by the Bidford ale-quaffers. After the prolonged drinking bout, the Bard settled down under a crab apple tree to sleep off the effects, to awaken some thirty-six hours later to pen the aforementioned lines. Exploring the descriptions of the other villages has exercised the imagination of many a folklorist since they first appeared in print in 1762.

The Cotswolds have inspired poets, songwriters and novelists on many different levels, providing as they do a picturesque background against which to set their thoughts and stories. Some authors, however, have disguised their homeland by changing the place names: John Moore's *Brensham Trilogy* is the most outstanding example depicting life in and around Tewkesbury; Reginald Arkell turned the Kempsford-Fairford area into a fictitious Merriford; Sir Compton Mackenzie's *Guy and Pauline* lived their novel life through the pages of Wychford for Burford, while the Victorian novelist, Dinah Maria Mulock, changed not only her characters' names and origins but also her own when she published *John Halifax, Gentleman* by 'Mrs Craik'.

T.S. Eliot used Burnt Norton as the title of one of his poems – but the name is genuine. The estate acquired its bizarre name from a disastrous fire started by the then owner, Sir William Keyte, a Member of Parliament for Warwick, who perished in it. Sir William was, by all accounts, a typical eighteenth-century rake, who had taken an innkeeper's daughter as his mistress and lived at Norton, on the escarpment between Chipping Campden and the Vale. After spending his considerable fortune on building the house and lovely gardens, all the while gradually sinking deeper into debt, replacing his mistresses one after the other and descending into an alcoholic all-time low, the fifty-three-year-old Keyte methodically set fire to a number of rooms with lighted candles on the night of 9 September 1741. A Campden scholar, George Ballard, described the event in a letter to his mother two days later:

> …I suppose you have heard of the dismal misfortune at Norton… a servant of Sir William Keyte's came riding furiously through the town, crying out that Norton House was on fire. I immediately ran thither, accompanied with a great number of people, and to my no small affliction, saw the greater part of that beautiful house in flames, which was the most terrible sight I ever beheld… smoke and flames… like Mount Etna… Sir William set it on fire himself, and voluntarily burnt himself in it, which was a dispatch too speedy for such a monster, who ought, like Lodowick Grevil, to have suffered death more leasurely [sic].

The loss of the grand building was mourned far more than the demise of Sir William – the spectacular suicide achieving for Norton a curious and tragic fame that has long outlived its infamous owner.

Thereby hangs a Tale

'Pretty, poor and proud' – Cheltenham has attracted more eloquent descriptions over the years: Edward VII, when Prince of Wales, said 'It would be difficult to find any part of England surpassing this neighbourhood in loveliness'; yet the dour old Radical, William Cobbett, penned his disapproval of the town when he visited it on his famous Rural Rides, as 'a nasty, ill-looking place, half clown, half cockney'. But a local maxim is always worth looking at in detail. Cheltenham is indeed pretty; a spread of Regency elegance on a terrace under the great bluff of Cleeve Hill, the highest point of the Cotswolds; the tree-lined Promenade has been regarded as the most beautiful thoroughfare in Britain. But poor? Certainly there is little evidence of poverty in this western gateway to the Cotswolds, rather the opposite could be said to be true, with its high-class shops, fashionable boutiques, art galleries, theatres and cultural festivals. Proud, it is rightly so. Cheltenham succeeded where many others failed. From its humble beginnings as a moderate little market town in constant competition with neighbouring Prestbury, each inhibiting the growth of the other, Cheltenham grew from what was no more than a single street (although it did stretch for almost a mile) in 1779.

To the three P's already discussed should perhaps be added a fourth – for Cheltenham, strangely, owes it success story to pigeons. In 1716 a meadow, where the famous Ladies' College now stands, was attracting an enormous number of pigeons to what turned out to be salt crystals at a spring. The owner railed round the spot, raised a thatched shed over it and gave the town its first pump-room. His astute son-in-law, Henry Skillicorne, built a more presentable edifice to house the spring in 1748, improved the approach to it and called it a 'Spa'. Physicians wrote learned treatises on the medicinal virtues of the waters, George III 'took' them and holidayed there for five weeks in 1788 and 'the favourite resort of fashion and the shrine of health' was developed as new wells were sunk, hundreds of visitors visited and the town put the pigeons in its coat of arms.

Cirencester, is often referred to as 'the capital of the Cotswolds'; as *Corinium* it was the second-largest city in Roman Britain and an important crossroads in its arterial system. Known as Cirencester from Saxon times – pronounced as Cisseter (in various forms of spelling) from the Middle Ages through to Shakespeare's day and lingering on in 'county' circles and venerable grandparents' speech – it was, in ancient times, according to William Worcestre writing in 1480, 'called the city of sparrows, because a certain Africanus, who came from Africa, destroyed the city after a siege by sending birds flying over the city with wildfire tied to their tails'.

Sparrows do not feature in any later history of the town, but the humble pigeon brought Cirencester not the commercial developments of the kind experienced at Cheltenham, but the proud distinction of supplying the first of its kind 'to be used with success for secret commu-

Kenley Lass, the Cirencester pigeon, with her Dicken medal for wartime service.

Chalford, once known as Neddyshire from the time deliveries could only be made by donkey cart.

nications from an Agent in enemy-occupied France while serving with the NPS [National Pigeon Service] in October 1940. Kenley Lass, bred by Donald Cole at the Bull Inn in Dyer Street, was Pigeon NURP 36 JH 190 in military circles, and completed her first mission of a flight home of some 300 miles in one day while carrying vital intelligence. She had remained hidden with her British Agent for eleven days following their parachute landing behind enemy lines. Kenley Lass was awarded the Dickin Medal, the animals' VC, for her bravery after a similar successful mission carried out in 1941.

Chalford's old name of Neddyshire derives from the time when deliveries could only be made by a sure-footed donkey. It is reckoned to be the second largest village in the country and rises from the Golden Valley floor in tier-upon-tier of twisting streets, with houses and cottages burrowed into the hillside, while others perch precariously over the edge. For over half a century, Jennie, the donkey, brought the village its daily bread in two huge pannier baskets. It was only through the insistence of the Fire Service that the street names were posted up in recent times – such was the close-knit nature of the community that everyone knew where to find everyone else.

Storybook names of the Stroud Valley

The Stroud Valley is punctuated with names that charmingly trip off the tongue like names from a storybook: the hamlets that make up Oakridge – Oakridge Lynch, Far Oakridge, Bournes Green, Water Lane, Iles Green and Tunley – have always been an enclave for writers, artists and craftsmen and individual spirits. Set somewhat apart from neighbouring villages, Oakridge earned the nickname of Little Russia or Little Siberia, indicating its rather isolated and elevated position. It has two village greens, the Village Green and Church Green, and a maze of footpaths, many of which have been named after local people – Joseph's Hill, Rebecca's Hill, Maria's Pitch, Twissels, Sammels and Back of Ollis. All are very evocative of how rooted the folk of the neighbourhood were in the places where they lived and worked.

Localised nomenclature appears in early legal documents, as shown in this extract from around 1240 translated from a medieval marriage settlement made for Henry de Olepenne, of Owlpen Manor, and Agnes de Bennecumbe:

Let those present and to come know that I, Walter de Bennecumbe, have given, granted, and by this my present charter confirmed to Henry, son of Sir Symon de Olepenne, with Agnes my daughter in free

marriage, all my land in Longelue which extends in length from Adam
le Stut's ditch to Peter de Ywelege's wood to have and to hold from
me and my heirs...

Long ago, local lore would have been necessary to find enchanting
Owlpen, that picturesque pocket of Cotswold Manor House steeped
in romance and mystery, with its court house, mill, barn and church
all nestled in its own little valley. The tale is still told of old Ferribee, a
local innkeeper of the distant past, giving these complicated directions
to strangers seeking the way to Owlpen.

> First you go down Fiery Lane until you come to Cuckoo Brook, then
> go to Horn Knep and round to Dragon's Den, carry on until you come
> to Potlid Green and so to Marling's End. If you keep straight on you will
> come right in to Olepen, but you must take care not to miss the road.

The old innkeeper told no lies, although it is just a mile from Uley.
Whichever way is taken, seeking out this enchanting place is well worth
the effort.

Brimscombe and Thrupp together form the parish of Thrupp – the
attractive hilly area where the valley road climbs from the old mill-
lined bottom steeply up to an area known locally as The Heavens.
Paradoxically, beyond Painswick on the A46 Cheltenham Road, you
have to go *down* to Paradise! Just how this idyllic wooded dell came
by its heavenly name is open to the interpretation of a number of
legends. The most popular and enduring is that Charles I, war-weary
and depressed from watching his army's defeat attempting to hold
Gloucester in the vale below, turned from his vantage point at
Painswick Beacon and sought refuge in the tiny hamlet folded into the
hill. The sanctuary and succour afforded the fugitive king there apparently prompted his remark, 'this is truly paradise'. Anyone disputing
this should be brave indeed, as history has proven – some ill-advised
body once tried to rename this spot, and an unholy local war broke out;
wiser folk would never have tried. Alas, the pub so appositely named
The Adam and Eve Inn – once upon a time kept by an innkeeper
called Abel! – called 'time' for the last time some years ago, but the ditty
(prompted by being served by Godsells Brewery of Salmon Springs)
lingers on:

> *Adam and Eve in Paradise*
> *God sells beer.*

Purgatory lies across the valley in *Cider with Rosie* country, below The Woolpack pub, where its author held court with the locals; the brewery has just launched a new beer – Laurie Lee's Bitter.

Valleys hereabouts contain names of sheer poetry – the Toadsmoor Valley – Valley of the Foxes – runs through Bismore, Kitlye, Cricketty and Nashend to Bisley, bordered by Maccus, Hawkley and Baker's Woods. The stream, springing from one of Bisley's Seven Wells (or Springs), winds its way under Swilley Bridge, past Cutham's Stile and through the Withey Bed, before filling Toadsmoor Lake. The flora and fauna of the countryside found their way into a number of place names – the much-maligned and persecuted badger perpetuates his nickname 'Brock' in Brockhampton and Brockworth, with the great loping hare making his appearance in Harescombe and Haresfield, whereas it is the garden leek which is credited with the root name of Leckhampton. Clapton-on-the-Hill in the North Cotswolds has now lost its strawberry fields, which lent it the summer-sounding name of 'Strawberry Village'.

Gustav Holst immortalised Cranham as the music for the words of 'In the Bleak Midwinter'; it is generally thought that it was composed while he was staying at Midwinter Cottage in the village where he sometimes played the church harmonium. Down Ampney was likewise immortalised – as the hymn tune to 'Come Down, O Love Divine' by Ralph Vaughan Williams, who was born at Down Ampney vicarage in 1872. He and Gustav Holst, who was born at Cheltenham, were the greatest of friends. When Vaughan Williams died in 1958, he was buried

The Vicarage at Down Ampney. Ralph Vaughan Williams immortalised Down Ampney, as a hymn tune composed as a tribute to his birthplace.

Whelford has neither well nor ford now, let alone the roadside stream that once fronted the (now closed) Queen's Head pub.

in Westminster Abbey, sealing his great standing in the country's cultural history; the music that accompanied the great composer to his last resting place was that commemorating his small rural Cotswold village birthplace – Down Ampney.

William Morris came late in his artistic life to the many-gabled Kelmscott Manor, where the 'Thames runs chill twixt mead and hill'. It was this Cotswold home he loved so much that he took as the name for his private press in Hammersmith – the Kelmscott Press.

Humps and Tumps, Barrows and Bottoms

Folklorists can have many a field day in exploring the origin and terrain of Cotswold's numerous tumps and bottoms and bends. Jackament and Tom Tit and Nanny Farmer and Waterley have their Bottoms, and the Fidler has his Elbow, while Cooper has his Hill. Belas has its Knap, while Jack and the Lad have their respective Barrows. Hetty Pegler and Nan Tow have their Tumps and Nags Head has both at Barrow Tump. Practically every walker of the Cotswold Way has crept into Hetty Pegler's Tump, a famous long barrow near Uley, an archaeological relic reckoned to be some 4,000 years old which takes its name from a seventeenth-century landowner.

Legend has it that Nan Tow was a witch who was buried standing upright in her tump. Molly Dreamer, so called from her conviction that her dreams of treasure hidden in the barrow at Gatcombe Lodge could become a reality if only she sought it, spent a great deal of her time digging for it there.

And Gladys Leaps to Join Them

The story of Gladys's Leap does not belong to the hoary past, but very much to the present day – but the tale of its becoming will now pass into folklore. Gladys Hillier was one of the fast-disappearing breed of post ladies who cycled their way through rain and shine taking written tidings to out-of-the-way places. For some thirty-five years Gladys delivered post in the widely-scattered parish of Cranham's steeply-wooded combs and crannies. Getting to one of the most isolated houses in her patch meant leaving her bicycle by a field gate along a country track, climbing the gate and burrowing her way through overhanging trees and tangled undergrowth, slipping and sliding down to the valley bottom (at least that is what I did when I followed the then just-retired Gladys to find her Leap).

Hardly another soul could have found the secret way through the wood to reach the field on the other side of the valley, so when the

Gladys with her Leap – officially named after her.

wooden plank that served as footbridge over the three-feet-wide stream at the bottom fell into disrepair there it stayed, eventually falling into the water to be swept away in the winter's rain. Undaunted by the little bridge too far gone to be of any further use, Gladys simply took a brave flying leap over the stream – not an easy thing to do by anybody's standards, let alone carrying a post bag and considering the slope of the facing bank, topped by a wooden stile into a field. There was still a steep incline to climb and another 'tidy step' to walk before the house could be reached. Then it was a quick turn around for a reverse order of slip, slide, leap and scramble through the shrubbery before she got back to her bike. Gladys's agility and dedication did not go unnoticed; when she retired the whole community rightly acknowledged her and, at the instigation of Mr Arthur Cooper of Haregrove House who wrote to the Ordnance Survey, the spot in the valley bottom she had so skilfully leapt across over the years was named after her.

The unusual honour of being accorded such recognition in one's own lifetime naturally caught the attention of the media at the time and Gladys admitted that she became heartily fed up with so much publicity. 'They had me leaping this way and that for the cameras for months', she recalled. However, she was very proud of the fact that a folk-song was dedicated to her prowess and happily signed hundreds of the record album sleeves of 'Gladys's Leap'.

Sounds of Foreign Influence

The two hamlets, Dunkirk and Petty France, look completely alien among our road signs to homely-sounding places with names derived from trades, crops, rivers and crafts. The names are generally attributed to the attempt to encourage Flemish weavers to establish their craft in the south Cotswolds. Likewise, Macaroni Woods and Farm and Downs, in the expanse of open country between Eastleach and Aldsworth, echo of earlier days when Bibury Races attracted the famous and the infamous in the late eighteenth century. The Macaroni Club members who frequented the races earned their name from their outlandish mode of dress, and foppish affectations, modelled it is said on the Italian playboys of the day. Some sources maintain that the area takes its name from the Derby winner, Macaroni, but the English Place Names Society records the name of Macaroni Farm in 1830 and it appears on property maps after that date, some considerable time before Macaroni – bred by the Marquis of Westminster at Eaton – won the Derby in 1863. The Bibury Race Club, however, still lives on in name and the main race meeting at Salisbury held at the beginning of July is known as the 'Bibury Meeting'.

Its peregrinations had taken it from Upton Downs, Burford, where it was founded in 1681 as the outcome of a visit by Charles II to Nell Gwynne while staying in the town, and it did a lot of travelling in the Cotswolds, before going over the county border to Wiltshire. In 1899, the Club took over the Salisbury racecourse.

Border Lines

If inter-village rivalries of the past were often a matter of local jealousies or parochial shows of strength or one-upmanship, they are as nothing to the feelings that are aroused by changing county borders and boundaries. One landmark that has now become a misnomer is the Four Shire Stone, the sturdy stone pillar fenced off beside the busy A44 between Moreton in Marsh and Chipping Norton. John Leland, Henry the Eighth's antiquary, wrote in 1520 while on a tour of Gloucestershire of '…a bigge Stone 3 Miles West from Rolleriche Stones; and standith yn a Hethe, bering the Name of Barton… This Stone is a very Marke or Limes of Glocestre, Wicestre, Warwicke and Oxfordeshires…'. The material and construction of the present stone is certainly of a later date, but its purpose is certainly historic, because now only three counties meet at that point since boundary changes took place.

A corner of Petty France.

Perhaps the last word lies with an old Gloucestershire shepherd, who was asked what he thought of bending the shire borders to fit more conveniently into county council administration. What would he think of becoming a Worcestershire man at a stroke of a bureaucrat's pen? The old shepherd gazed northward from his Cotswold hill top, and said, 'Oh, no. No I don't like the thoughts o' that – they d'say it be colder in Woostashur. These Cotsalls, they be much cosier in Glaastershur'.

3
COUNTRY CURES

We would look askance today if a lady pulled out of her pocket a frog's foot with her lacy hanky, so it seems somewhat incongruous that in the days when females had a fit of the vapours on the least whim, they hung quite repulsive objects about their person 'to cure all the complaints no-one has ever died of', to coin an old Cotswold phrase. But in the days when medical help was sought only for the chronically sick, the dying or for an ailing family pig, day-to-day ailments and afflictions were treated with the flora and fauna of the countryside and a lot of faith in the old wives' tales. Many folk remedies have since been proven to have genuine medicinal properties; often, however, the treatments were rather worse than the complaints, but highly interesting for their place in social history.

The majority of beliefs in the cure-alls have been handed down by oral tradition: 'they always said that…' – quite who the original *they* were is lost in the mists of time, but *they* weave a fascinating thread throughout our folklore fabric – it was the obscure, omnipotent '*they*' who said that to carry a nutmeg in one pocket and a frog's foot in the other was an insurance to ward off rheumatism. In fact, *they* appear to have had a dread of rheumatism, warts, lovesickness and the ague in equal measure.

Country folk of yesteryear: souls of the soil, mainly uneducated but learned in lore and the ways of life.

Among the many preventative precautions against rheumatism you could choose from included soaking your hands and feet in boiled elder-flowers, eating boiled young nettles, or thrashing yourself all over with stinging nettles. I recall seeing old Grampy Wallington of Lechlade flailing his lower arms with nettles when I was a child; he always appeared to be *sprack* and lively, so I assume it worked for him.

Bee stings were also recommended and still are. Many years ago I asked Wilfred Smith, one of Daglingworth's oldest inhabitants and a tenant of the Duchy of Cornwall who had bought much of the village, if he had met his royal landlord. He said:

> Lor, oh, ah. Came to the hall – as was then. A-comes up to I a'ter ee'd sin t'others and axed what I did do. Told un I were gardener at the Rectory till I got sort of crocked up with the rheumaticks. 'Knows a good cure for that,' the Prince zays – 'bee-stings!' Your 'ighness, I zays. I've a-kept bees for forty year and they 'asn't cured I yet. Laugh, I never yeard a young chap laugh as 'earty as that.'

Bees figure large in the annals of folklore and have been part of the culture of civilisations throughout the ages. An old Cotswold jingle conjures up their importance in the interdependence of country life and living:

Wilfred Smith of Daglingworth recounts to a neighbour a visit from his royal landlord, Prince Charles.

> *Sheep for clover and clover for bees*
> *Wool and honey from clover leyes*
> *Sheep for wool and wool for wealth*
> *Bees for honey and honey for health*
> *This is what was said of old*
> *On the hills of Cotteswold*

Honey features in two of the wonderful remedies – 'receipts' in my grandmother's notebook – which, judging by the dates, must have been passed down to her. Reading the beautiful copperplate writing brings to life the agonies and discomfiture of pre-antibiotic days and the ingenuity of our forebears in trying to alleviate the pain and distress of so many conditions:

Mastoids – plaister for Mothers (dated 1845)
A tablespoonful of sweet oil, a tablespoonful of honey, the yolk of a new laid egg. Mix these well together and then add flour till it is a thick batter. Spread this very thickly on a cloth, warm it a little before the fire. Then place the cloth over the whole breast leaving a large hole for the milk to pass through.

The ingredients in the second remedy again read as something more suited for a cooking pan than for slapping on one's body:

As many country cures were produced in the potting shed as the Elizabethan lady's still room.

Honey Poultice for Broken Breasts or Inflammation
Equal parts of honey and sweet oil and sherry wine. Simmer them together
until melted, then add dried flour until it is a soft paste. Spread it on linen
and apply at night and morning for a gathered breast and once a day when
it continues easy.
From Aunt Lloyd

Between the materials and methods recorded for Mrs Howard's
Orange Jelly, Preserving Eggs in Quick Lime – with notes on 'how to
make fowls pay' and 'Washing and Starching Collars and Cuffs', I found
the following 'receipt':

For Rheumatism
Camphor ¾oz. Ox gall ½ pint. Spirits of Wine ½ pint. Dissolve the camphor
in the spirits of wine. Add the gall warm from the animal. Shake it well.

Great Grandma added a note that the 'receipt' came from Mrs Fawcett
Weston. There is no indication as to whether it worked or, indeed,
whether the resulting concoction was imbibed or rubbed on; perhaps it
was too difficult to decipher whether it was the mixture or the animal
that was to be shaken well!

The Housewives Lewis of yore were well armed through the wisdom and advice gleaned and garnered from friends and relatives – most acknowledged by name – to deal with generations of sprains and colic and 'disagreeable bowels', whooping cough and threadworms and a whole array of fevers and melancholic maladies, thanks to the little black book. And where the cure was not instant, there are numerous receipts for nutritious 'food for the invalid', including the 'most excellent beef tea' culled from *The Lancet*. There is even a receipt for making laudanum, that all-powerful dope of yesteryear; very simply made it was too, according to the book – simply dissolve half an ounce of opium in four ounces of brandy! It features largely, of course, in all the sedative mixtures and even in one to rub on bad bruises.

Beauty preparations did not go much further than 'clearing the skin' and 'watching the bowels' but there are two receipts for hair oil:

Take unsalted hogs lard 2 oz
Purified trotters oil 1 oz
Essence of Bergamot, a few drops
Oil of lavender [ditto]
and the same of Otto of Roses.
Wash the lard well with rose water and be very careful to have it fresh!

Receipts for ailments and making furniture polish, including one for Nose Bleed, 'from Ashley Cooper for Thomas Fox, 1808'.

The second, simply titled 'Another', uses bone marrow, melted, poured into a basin of water and adding salad oil before putting into a pipkin. The smell could be sweetened 'with any perfume you think best' before potting. The delight of 'Another' receipt to me is the use of the word pipkin – conjuring up the world of Beatrix Potter, when through her pen she had the Tailor of Gloucester sending his cat, Simpkin, into the streets of the city with his 'last groat and a china pipkin to buy a penn'orth of bread, a penn'orth of milk and a penn'orth of sausages'.

In a later (also black) notebook between the pattern for a 'Gent's Knitted Tie' and 'Mrs Lee's recipe for Tomato Pickle', dated 1932, 'pence worth' instead of weight or measure is given for (presumably a cure for) Lumbago:

4 penny worth of Copathia
2 penny worth of Juniper
2 penny worth of Sweet Nitre
10 drops on a lump of sugar twice a day.

Old women have been famous for curing warts since Lucian's time, and the remedies tend to be appropriately drastic, and in some cases downright macabre. For example, rubbing your hands together while facing a new moon can only be effective if you then make haste to the nearest gallows and pass a hanged person's hand over the warts.

A Gloucestershire newspaper report of 1777 stated that 'after he [Dr Dodd] had hung about ten minutes, a very decently dressed young woman went up to the gallows in order to have a wen on her face stroked by the doctor's hand.' *The Times* of 26 August 1819 gave a similar story: 'after the body had hung for some time, several persons applied for permission to rub the hand of the deceased over their wens'.

If your neighbourhood ridded itself of its gallows then you could steal – they definitely specified *steal* – 'a piece of beef from a butcher's shop, rub it over the offending warts, then throw it down the necessary house; as the beef rots so your warts disappear!'

Elias Ashmole recorded in his diary of 1681 how he took a good dose of elixir, then hung three spiders about his neck – and they drove the ague away. '*Deo gratias*' he added. Something must have driven the ague out of our repertoire of maladies, that all-embracing, shivering fever that so afflicted our forefathers, unless we can include our common cold and influenza as modern-day equivalents; but seeking a cure for the common cold is still exercising the time and talents of researchers today. But, to take heart, Hippocrates himself advocated sneezing to cure the hiccups and 'to be profitable in lethargies, apoplexies and catalepsies!'

Toothache was eased by wrapping the face up in a sheet of brown paper that had first been sprinkled with vinegar, pepper and salt (obviously not any old fish-and-chip wrapper). If the household's only sheet of brown paper had been used 'to mend a crown' in true Jack and Jill nursery rhyme tradition, then a common old garden cabbage leaf would make a good substitute, but it had to be quickly blanched before seasoning. If the thought of waking up with a cold, wet cabbage leaf sticking to your face did not appeal, then you had the option of chewing a plug of baccy, or rolling a piece of corrugated cardboard into a spill, lighting it and inhaling the smouldering vapour. When all charms and cures failed then it was off to the village blacksmith to remove the offending tooth! Babies' teething pains were eased by placing a silver three penny piece under the pillow, or a cheaper alternative was to dry the roots of the deadly nightshade and string the pieces together for the child to wear around its neck.

Rickety-limbed children were once subjected to the discomfiture of being passed naked through the aperture made by cleaving a young tree down its trunk; afterwards the tree was bound round, so as to make it unite, in the belief that as the tree grew together so the child acquired new strength. The slime from snails made a more repugnant, but less physically demanding cure. Brimstone and treacle were doled out on bath nights to keep the skin clear of spots; raw carrots were eaten to improve the eyesight and children were cajoled into eating their bread crusts to make their hair curl.

Gretton grannies were criticised by a church warden of the parish in 1891 when he discovered they were 'curing' young children of whooping cough by pulling them under a briar, rooted at both ends, at dawn on three consecutive mornings.

Some Victorian families firmly believed in the insulating properties of goosegrease. Granny Morse at Little Faringdon Railway Crossing remembered some of her contemporaries being 'sewn up' for winter: a thick layer of goosegrease was spread over the child's back and chest, large patches of brown paper were then stuck on to the unctuous mess, and a flannel body shape was stitched over the top to keep it all in place until spring crept over the windowsill. I was told by Annie Tinney of Leafield Farm, Quenington, that she remembered how any fat left over from protecting the children from likely ills and chills was used by her father to grease the farm wagon and cart wheels.

Dawn Dew was the mystical term for the simplest cure for asthma. You just had to lie down at dawn break in the damp dew on the grass where Cotswold sheep have been sleeping all night. After all, who ever heard of sheep suffering from asthma? Of course, if you caught your death of cold curing the asthma it would be difficult to prove its effectiveness!

A trio of Victorian children, prettified for a studio photograph.

Among the 'Collects and Creed', 'Reflections on Marriage' and 'Observations on Pinder's Observations', Hester Keble of Fairford wrote her eighteenth-century 'Receipt for an Asthma':

My good old friend – accept from me the following rules without a fee:
An asthma is your case I think, so you must neither eat nor drink
I mean of Meat preserv'd in Salt, or any Liquor made of Malt.
From season'd Sauce avert your eyes from Ham and Tongue and pidgeons pyes.

If venison patty is sett before you, each bite you eat Memento Mori
Your supper Nothing if you please, but above all no toasted cheese.
Tis likely you will now observe what I prescribe will make you starve
No – I allow you at a Meal a leg, loyn or neck of Veal
Young turkeys I allow you four, partridge or pullets half a score.
Of house lamb boyld eat quarters two, the devil's in it if that won't doe.

Now as to liquor, why indeed, what I advise – I send you Mead.
Glass's of this to extinguish drought, take three with water, three without.
Lett Constant exercise be tried – sometimes walk and sometimes ride
Health oftener comes from Blackdown Hill than from the apothecary's bill.

For breakfast it is my advice eat gruel, sago, barley, rice.
Take burdock roots and by my troth I'd mingle Daisies in my broth.
Thus may you draw with ease your breath eluding long the dart of death.
Thus may you laugh; look clear and thrive, enrich'd by those whom you survive.

Grandma Keble, also of Keble House (but known at that time as Court Close), the home of the Revd John Keble, celebrated poet-divine, advocated Toast Water as a general aid to digestion. Her recipe was much less poetic and quite prosaic: simply pour boiling water over well-scorched toasted bread, leave to steep for two hours, then strain through muslin and flavour with a sliver of lemon or orange peel.

The beggarly drink of Crust Water was part of the diet of Dursley paupers in the town's workhouse, but the allowance of the pound of bread required to make it was the subject of an inquiry by the Workhouse Committee in November 1839. It was finally decided that the 'established custom' could continue.

Clergymen's wives were the fount of all well-tested, tried and true tonics and potions. Whole hamlets and homesteads in and around Cold Aston and the Rissingtons were cured of their cuts and bruises, bumps and lumps by 'Nora Cheales's Aunt Mary's Ointment':

2 ozs beeswax, cut up small
2 ozs white powdered resin
2 ozs butter straight from the churn
Mix all together over a gentle heat and pour into china pots.

The Oxfordshire Cotswold villagers at Leafield exercise their right to enter Wychwood Forest each Palm Sunday to make Spanish Water. The reputedly miraculous spring water of Wychwood was mixed with Spanish liquorice and lemon to make a cure-all to last the entire year. Bathing the eyes in Holy Water – rainwater caught on holy days, such as Easter and the many Saints' days – was always particularly valued. Best of all was the water that 'ran against the sun'; few rivers run west to east, but the waters at Langley Hill do, so Winchcombe folk should have had well-sighted ancestors.

A south-running stream is the only one to lie alongside to ease the aches and pains of sciatica and chant this little ditty. But first, you must know that the old Cotswold name for sciatica is 'boneshave', so that is why you sing this while lying on the damp river bank:

Boneshave right, boneshave straight
As the water runs by the stave
So follows boneshave.

of ivy was made into drinking cups in ancient times to cure alcoholics – due to the bitterness of the wood. Ground ivy was commonly called 'Old Ale-Hoof', from the time the hoof-shaped leaves were used to clear and improve the taste of home-brewed ale.

Herbal remedies are still very much in use today as more and more people turn to alternative medicine rather than drugs. The irritation from insect bites is said to be eased by binding the leaves of yarrow, birdsfoot trefoil or plaintain over the affected parts. Insomniacs stick to the 'sleep pillows', filled with lavender and/or hops, that are so hugely popular in gift shops. Comfrey, still known as 'knit-bone' to country-folk, was once widely used to mend fractured limbs in pre-plaster of Paris days. The roots of the plant were crushed, then laid on leather and bound round the injured part. Tea made from its leaves was used to ease chest complaints. Garlic crushed in home-made lard was rubbed on the soles of feet in an effort to cure 'Brown Kitties' (bronchitis), while hardier folk smoked dried coltsfoot and bramble leaves to relieve the symptoms! According to one chronicler, possibly Fosbroke, grammar schools in Gloucestershire actually taught smoking! It is said that after tobacco had come into general use, the children carried pipes in their satchels which their mothers took care to fill, so that 'it might serve instead of breakfast. At the accustomed hour everyone laid aside his book and lit his pipe, the master smoking with the boys and teaching them how to hold their pipes, and draw in the tobacco. At this era people even went to bed with their pipe in their mouth, and got up in the night to light it'! Marshmallow leaves were doubly useful, both as a poultice and as an infusion in hot milk or water as a medicine to reduce any inflammation of the body. The pain from a burnt finger tip was eased by pressing it to the lobe of the ear.

A plea through the *Cotswold Life Magazine* a few years ago asking for any tried and true cures for night cramps brought me an interesting clutch of replies – the effectiveness of the cures all verified by tales of kinfolk 'never having them after'. There was an exception in a friend's father-of-a-friend who, after successfully curing his nocturnal misery by placing an old potato in his bed, had the talisman confiscated when he took it to hospital. Despite his suffering again with night cramps while he was there, he was not allowed his strange bedfellow. Another sworn-by cure was that of sleeping with a bag of corks under the mattress.

A potato carried in the pocket is said to ward off rheumatism, while an onion warded off sickness and plague. A small onion, roasted in the oven, and put inside the ear while just warm has proved effective in alleviating earache. Peony seeds, dried and threaded into a necklace, should be worn more as an amulet against, rather than a cure for, lunacy.

It is said that pipe-smoking was actually taught at one time in some Gloucestershire grammar schools. Smoking or pipe meetings were popular up until the thirties, when this photo was taken in the Mill Inn, Withington.

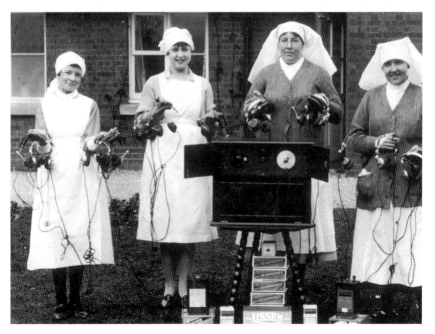

Hospitals were financed by local subscription and fund-raising. Here, matron, sister and nurses of Fairford Hospital (built in 1887 and the smallest cottage hospital in Gloucestershire), proudly show its first wireless set, complete with headphones, bought by the local WI in the early thirties.

An infallible 'Cure for the Bite of a Mad Dog' is preserved in the archives of the County Record Office. Sir George Cobb, Bart, who brought the recipe from Tonquin, testified that 'This medicine has been given to hundreds with success and (he) himself has cured Two Persons who had the Symptoms of Madness upon them'. Given to the person as soon as possible after the bite, the concoction comprised 'Native Cinnabar, Fictitious Cinnabar and Musk' ground into an exceedingly fine powder and mixed with 'Arrack, Rum or Brandy'.

Spirits and ale feature prominently in a vast number of the old 'receipts' and remedies. Gout, traditionally linked with excessive wining and dining since Roman times, reared its painful head at Bourton-on-the-Water in the early 1970s. When the village was reported as having the nation's highest number of gout sufferers, the media swarmed in the wake of mobile laboratories and all the old cures were given an airing, the least obnoxious of which was the wearing of a sheepskin vest. Earlier gouty grandparents would have perhaps found a bramble, rooted at both ends, and struggled under its arching branch even if it was more in good faith than reason. However, the *New Scientist* pointed out at the time (after gently railing the press for its humorous treatment of the painful news), there was always St Sebastian to pray to – the patron saint of gout!

4
Ghosts, Witches
& Other Goings-On

Mists gather swiftly over the high, lonely sheep-walks of the upper wolds, and linger in the secluded dips and dells of the valleys, seemingly fusing distance and time together, distorting the familiar scene. In such conditions echoes no longer ring out clearly through the trees, but drop hushed and heavy, like damp leaves to the ground, and trees, buildings and stone walls can seem suddenly to lack substance. Could it have been at such times that Shakespeare trod these ways and was inspired to create Ariel, with his plaintive songs of the spirit, and Puck, plucked straight out of Elizabethan folklore? It is easy to see how shapes might become shadows and old tales tantalise the imagination.

Poets' flights of fancy have always been connected to the consideration of folktales; elements of Shakespeare's most magical creation, *A Midsummer Night's Dream,* are, according to at least one academic, 'in some way indebted to Chaucer's *Knight's Tale'* – amongst a handful of other ancient sources, including *Scot's Discovery of Witchcraft.* Certainly, the Cotswolds were familiar ground to William Shakespeare. So, too, would have been the lore, language and legends of the Cotswolds. Sprites and spirits, ghosts and witches weave throughout his best-loved plays. It is interesting to think of the great bard culling ideas from Chaucer inasmuch as Chaucer also spent time, in an earlier age, in and around the Cotswolds. He was at

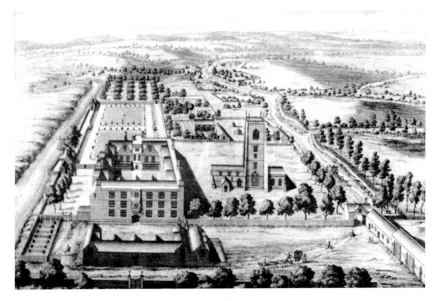

Kempsford – one of the country's most haunted villages.

Kempsford, under the patronage of Blanche, the Plantagenet heiress who married John of Gaunt in 1359, and Kempsford is perhaps the strongest contender for being the most haunted Cotswold village.

Kynemeresford, to give quiet Kempsford its ancient name, is a small village settled on the Gloucestershire side of the Thames where it runs deep and chill between whispering waterweeds, separating it from Wiltshire – the boundary over which the ancient kingdoms of Wiccii fought the Walsati. Spectres from those Saxon days have lingered long in Cotswold folklore, such as old Oswyn, remorsefully shaking his white head, who is said to keep eternal watch over his beautiful, golden-haired Ina, the ward whom he tried and failed to defend from the lustful advances of the pagan warrior Hengstan. It was from the castle tower that Oswyn spied on the young lovers through an arrow shaft. He banished young Ina to her bower while his guards beat the daring Norseman senseless and bound him with ox-hide straps to a wild horse. Whipped through the ford, the horse sped crazily over the Wiltshire fields and dropped dead from exhaustion at nightfall. But not so the brave Hengstan; bruised and battered, but by no means broken, he sheltered in the Walsatian dales and joined their warriors. Seeking revenge, Hengstan stole back to Kempsford in a bark boat which he hid among the water iris, scaled the castle wall and led the assault of the Walsati on the Wiccii stronghold. Hengstan's heroic feats won not only the battle, but the fair hand of Ina and a place in the history of the riverbank hauntings.

The river hereabouts is famously restless with many spectral souls, including those of two Lady Mauds, to add to the confusion. The senior spirit is that of Lady Maud, heiress of the noble house of Chaworth. She was betrothed by licence of Edward I, who held his royal court at Kempsford Castle, but her child groom did not reach maturity and Maud was married instead to Henry, Duke of Lancaster, who succeeded to the Barony of Kempsford in 1336. Their only son drowned in the ford – from which the village was named. The duke, esteemed throughout Europe as a 'perfect knight', could not face life within sight of the waters that had robbed him of his young heir, and abandoned his wife and home to their tragic memories. A shoe, cast by his horse as he rode away, was picked up by the villagers and nailed to the church door. It is still there. And Lady Maud is still there, too, in spirit. As moonlight silvers the sedge-edged water, it is said that her soft sighs and sometimes spine-chilling cries can be heard along the riverbank as she wills her young son to return.

But it is the second Lady Maud, the Lady of the Mists, who really holds centre stage in the dramatic tales of this riverbank. As the light of day dissolves to dusk, the fog-drenched air above the dark waters of the Thames rises wraith-like, as Lady Maud emerges cold and pale to keep her nightly tryst. Her story dates back to the period of the Barons' uprising against Edward II. Like many a family divided by civil strife, her husband and brother were on opposing sides. One storm-swept night her brother arrived at the castle seeking refuge; her husband was away at the wars and Maud was able to hide her brother in a secret room at the foot of the battlements bounding the river. A knight of the household, whose amorous advances she had repeatedly spurned, took it into his head to spy on her and, upon hearing a man's voice coming from the stony cell where she had gone under cover of darkness, sought revenge on the lovely Maud by sending a message to her husband to the effect that she was having a clandestine affair.

Enraged at the news, husband Henry returned home without Maud's knowledge and followed her to the small riverine room. Blinded by outrage and jealousy, Henry struck down the man, then caught Maud up in his arms and threw her over the battlement wall into the Thames. When the truth emerged of Maud giving succour and shelter to her brother, secreting him away because of civil war, the jealous knight became a penitent monk. Meanwhile, Lady Maud began haunting her hasty husband and no doubt kept the knight's soul from eternal rest beneath his sculpted statue in the church chancel, perhaps explaining his reputed clanking trips up the riverbank to the Old Vicarage.

Lady Maud's Walk, a grassed terrace rampart in the remains of the old castle, is named after this Lady Maud. It was the only place where the

Kempsford Old Vicarage – home to a whole host of ghosts.

Ancient ramparts alongside Lady Maud's Walk.

local Home Guard doubled up for night patrol during the Second World War. Defence against the known enemy is one thing; chancing across the Lady Maud in the pale moonlight would make many a brave man tremble beneath his tin helmet!

The Old Vicarage, built in the old castle precincts, is home to most of the ghosts of Kempsford. The two Mauds wail and weave their way along the riverbank at the bottom of the garden and overlook the tennis court from Lady Maud's Walk, and the miserable monk mumbles penitent prayers in the passage. But it is the 'Blue Boy' who has become the resident phantom guest in the drawing room. A young boy, dressed in what has been described as a blue velvet 'Bubbles' suit, is reported to sit in a winged chair – even though such a chair is not part of the present furnishings! The ghost could well be that of a youthful Lord Coleraine, who owned the great house after it was rebuilt from the ancient castle in the time of James I. George Hanger, or Lord Coleraine, a Regency rake known as 'Blue Hanger' due to his passion for blue clothes, language and manners, paid off his gambling debts by dismantling the mansion house and selling the stone to build Buscot Park. According to his own instructions, he was buried above ground to prevent the devil from snatching him – but later Victorians put him away tidily under the organ at St Mary's church, Driffield. David Verey, the eminent architectural historian, thought that the church had been rebuilt in 1734 by the first Lord Coleraine.

A far more humble spirit is that of a nursemaid in eighteenth-century dress who carries a baby down the servants' staircase.

Appropriately, it was on the eve of Halloween some years ago that I went again to the Old Vicarage, reputedly England's most haunted house, to check the spectral score. It was home at that time to the Mahoney family, and little Katy Mahoney walked with me along Lady Maud's Walk to the ruins of the little river room. Back in the warmth of the kitchen, young Matthew Mahoney told me of the tall man with short hair, wearing a high black hat and long coat, whom he had seen walking in the back corridor and, later that same evening, across Katy's room and out through the wall. I considered this to be very detailed for nine-year-old fancy; he had remembered every detail over two years, and he was a most convincing witness.

So, I checked with Hilary, comparing her children's experiences to those well-documented in local lore. Was it nine or ten ghosts? Did the knight-turned-monk count as one or two spirits, as he had been seen in both guises; should the baby in the nursemaid's arms be reckoned as a separate ghostly being? Hilary wasn't sure either, she adopted the philosophical view that such an ancient site must hold spirits of a long past and felt that the Old Vicarage was a little like Motley Hall. With so many ghosts floating about it is a wonder they don't all collide, but when the Mahoneys held their family parties, so did the subjects of their own ghost stories – upstairs in the attic they could be heard making their own distinctive bumps in the night.

Later, from another source, I was told that on occasions when the Old Vicarage had guests, the 'Blue Boy' had been seen, still sitting in his chair, down the road at the Manor Farmhouse, which was built on the site of the twelfth-century castle. And to refer to an even earlier age, the tramp of marching feet and the confused sounds of conflict heard not so long ago in this decade by a couple of villagers coming from the corner of the road by the church could have come across the wavelength of the centuries since the Wiccii fought the Walsati. Sceptics will explain the bumps in the night hereabouts to the proximity of Fairford Airbase, the test ground of Concorde and now world-renowned as the home of the International Air Tattoo. Aerodynamic physicists dismiss them as refracted sound waves from the base, having similarly explained away the cannon shots of the Dutch sea battle which Samuel Pepys recorded in 1666. But the sights and sounds of the supernatural here were locked into the legend of the land long before the age of supersonic.

It is no surprise when searching for ghostly goings-on to find that the Cotswolds have more ghosts per acre than other regions. But what is a ghost?

Many years ago I asked the question of my dear friend, the late Canon Harry Cheales, Rector of Wyck and Little Rissington. Canon Cheales had listened to more ghost stories than anyone, not as entertainment but as a priest designated by the Diocese to exorcise buildings and sites where a supernatural presence and troublesome happenings have disturbed people.

> A ghost has not flesh and blood. This is the definition given by Jesus Christ, who proved to his friends that he was not a ghost by allowing them to touch him, and by eating fish and honeycomb. I have met ghosts which could be seen and have spoken, but never any that could be touched or could eat.

Replying to my questions as to whether there was good reason for people to be afraid of encountering a ghost, he explained:

> Fear is an emotion brought about by anything unexpected or unexplained, for this very reason most people are afraid of ghosts. We have a built-in warning when in the presence of evil – you feel cold and your hair stands

Canon Harry Cheales, Rector of Wyck Rissington, was an acknowledged authority on ghostly goings-on.

on end, but such ghosts are rare; most are quite harmless and even protective. A good example of this is in the Bible; those to whom the angels appeared are all described as 'being afraid'. I know there are sceptics, but even the most hard-bitten sceptic has admitted to experiencing manifestations, especially poltergeist activities. All poltergeists are ghosts; it is a German word meaning 'a ghost that throws', it doesn't appear to have any human agency. A poltergeist is really a mischievous spirit with little intelligence and an animal type of nature. The circus fraternity maintain that they are the ghosts of chimpanzees! What we usually mean by 'a ghost' is the spirit of a human being.'

I was keen to know whether what I had heard, or read in the far-off past, about a ghost having no power to speak until it is spoken to first, and the correct mode of addressing a spectre was to command it in the name of the three persons of the Trinity to tell who it is and its business, was true.

With years of experience dealing with dozens of different types of hauntings, Canon Cheales again turned to the Scriptures for illustration:

This reminds me of the Mount of Transfiguration when St Peter broke the spell by speaking and the Virgin faded. This often happens when people are bold enough to speak to apparitions, whether it stops them completing

The wealth of historic hostelries in the Cotswolds abound with tales of the appearances and capers of various 'things that go bump in the night'. Unfortunately space does not permit more than a random selection of these fascinating phantom folk, who have added their own characters to our folklore heritage.

To begin in our shire city, Gloucester's New Inn, built in 1455 by Abbot John Twining to accommodate the tourist trade in pilgrims to the tomb of Edward II, has a white-robed resident wraith in the Queen's Suite and ghost-riders in the courtyard, according to reports of the clattering of hooves heard at around midnight. This inn has a fascinating history; legend has it that Shakespeare himself once appeared in one of the plays performed in the courtyard, and Lady Jane Grey was staying at the inn in 1553 when she was pronounced Queen of England. And one could see the 'Corsican Fairy', the 2 ft 10 inch tall Maria Theresa, here in the eighteenth century, along with a mermaid said to have been captured off the coast of Mexico, but these wondrous females were human exhibits for which one had to pay 6d to view.

The former Archdeacon Street School had its ghost in 'Charlie', visible only to children, who described him as an old, white-haired man with gown and mortarboard, who watched them and smiled. Charlie was

Gloucester city holds many a ghost in its long past.

somewhat less benign to the adults who worked there – paint and tins were upset in a locked room during re-decorating and a shovel hit a caretaker of its own accord. Research into these unexplained happenings revealed that a teacher had died there after falling down some stone steps. The hauntings carried out by a young nun carrying a child, who it seemed had died while under her care during the time that Gambier Parry Lodge was a children's hospital, seem to have ceased since it was demolished, but not before the workmen engaged in razing the Victorian building had experienced enough of the unseen presence to decide to work in pairs.

No. 120 Westgate Street also lost its hooded monk when the building was pulled down, but whether it is a courteous monk who has given visitors a hand with putting on their coat in the Bishop's House is difficult to assess – since the hand is invisible! Dogs are particularly susceptible to the paranormal and they are recorded as being completely terrified of a room above St Mary's archway – the room overlooked the burning at the stake of Bishop Hooper in 1555. The Old Bell Inn, formerly the Epicure, in busy Southgate Street, hit the headlines in the local press in 1975 when the chef of its newly opened restaurant was woken by the frightening apparition of an old, silver-haired crone in a long white nightdress sitting on his bed – only to disappear before he gathered enough breath to shout for help. The spectre was seen by several customers around that time and a reporter, hot on the trail of the ghostly goings-on at the Old Bell, witnessed for himself the eerie pouring out of a glass of beer from a tap moving slowly downward – with no-one anywhere near the bar at the time.

Tewkesbury has its share of inns and hotels where poltergeist activities have been freely but reliably recounted, with the odd sighting, sounds and sensations. Many, like in most other hostelries in the Cotswolds, are either discounted or cherished as part of the fabric of the place and landlords, managers and proprietors tend to either give them an airing or closet them away according to the nervous or otherwise disposition of their customers, clients or guests. No mention of Tewkesbury would be complete without a reminder of its historic role in the decisive battle in the closing years of the protracted War of the Roses, and indeed one hotel has inherited a 500-year-old soldier ghost, who had dragged himself to one of its rooms to die after being wounded on the town's aptly named Bloody Meadow.

Our once lonely highways and byways were the favourite haunts of highwaymen, their crimes often romanticised in retrospect as a kind of socially justified redistribution of riches. Few, in reality, were of the legendary Dick Turpin type and most were no more than notorious

Tewkesbury, a town of secret alleyways.

muggers on horseback. Many an inn has been forced to give shelter to a pursued pistol-wielding rider, bringing disquiet to those that might see or hear the unwelcome guest. Some hostelries even trade under the name. The Highwayman on the Gloucester (old Roman Ermine Street) Road has a splendid coach securely fixed to its forecourt, so it cannot have been that which has been seen, drawn by four white horses, speeding across the road to disappear in the Syde direction – as witnessed by several drivers at different times in this last decade.

The Highwayman at Burford, which was old when the first Queen Elizabeth was young, boasts not a cloak and dagger villain as its resident ghost, but a young Victorian woman in a frilled white apron who spends her time there ascending the stairs in the most demure manner. The only highwayman connection to the hotel seems to be back in the eighteenth century when the Hunt family owned the former inn and traded there in ironmongery. One James Hunt, who became a notable surgeon and pioneer of smallpox inoculation, sent an armed highwayman packing when he was travelling on the lonely road between Burford and Northleach.

The A40, an old coach road from Cheltenham to Oxford and on to London, was, in Canon Cheales's experienced opinion, probably the most haunted highway in the country. This thoroughfare has long been infamous for road accidents – quite a number of which have been blamed on the sudden appearance of a coach and four dashing across the road, causing drivers to brake or swerve violently with disastrous consequences.

Dan the Duke is the name given to the ghost of a highwayman with an arrow in his back, who died on the doorstep of the Puesdown on the A40. The inn has been the scene of many unexplained noises and happenings over the years, from bottles rising from crates of their own volition to basin taps being turned on while someone was in the shower. The age of the inn also remains something of a mystery, although historians have made a calculated guess at thirteenth-century origins. In 1995 the Puesdown became The Cotswold Explorer. The new owners changed the name in honour of Cheltenham-born Antartic explorer Edward Wilson, who perished with Scott on his ill-fated mission to the South Pole in 1912.

The most notorious highwaymen of the Cotswolds were a far cry from your ordinary Tom, Dick or Harry. Reckless and ruthless, the Dunsdon brothers terrorised the London to Oxford coaching route and around the

Stagecoaches were a romantic if rough and dangerous mode of transport, prey of the notorious highwaymen.

Capps Lodge was the haunt of Cotswold's most infamous highwaymen – Tom, Dick and Harry.

Wychwood Forest area in the eighteenth century. Tom, Dick and Harry Dunsdon were of a respectable Fulbrook family and when they had turned to crime on the highway they favoured the Bird in Hand Inn at Capps Lodge, just outside Burford. One night they attempted a break-in at Tangley Manor as a change from holding up stagecoaches. When Dick put his arm through the shutter of the front door to grab the key it was seized by a couple of the Manor staff and the local constable, who had been tipped off by someone who had overheard the brothers' plan. The men inside the hall swiftly tied Dick's hand to the iron handle. Then they recoiled in horror as the cry 'Cut, cut' came from outside, followed by piercing screams and Dick's arm falling through the door shutter to swing on the handle inside. A pool of blood was all that was to be seen outside as the sound of galloping horses died away. Any posse set up to follow the hoof prints was bound to be foiled as the highwaymen had their horses shod with round shoes by a Fifield blacksmith who, no doubt, was too petrified by their swaggering demands to refuse the job.

Dick presumably died from the effects of having his arm severed so dramatically by his brothers, as he was never seen with them again. That is, not in the flesh – reports of a ghost appearing by the gibbet tree close by the old inn where Tom and Harry hung in chains after being hanged at Gloucester in 1784 specified that it had but one arm. The eventual downfall of the infamous Dunsdons took place back at their old haunt, the Bird in Hand, where they were revelling with the crowds gathered for the Burford Whitsuntide festival. After gambling and drinking the night away, a quarrel broke out and Harry fired point blank at William Harding, the landlord. A 'ha'penny' in his waistcoat pocket deflected the bullet and saved his life. Others joined in the fray and overpowered the Dunsdon brothers and they were arrested. A string of charges was brought against them and after their execution their bodies returned to the Cotswolds and became such a tourist attraction of the day that eventually they were removed from the gibbet and buried beneath the trees by Capps Lodge. Someone had carved the initials TD and HD and the date on the tree and their infamy turned to fame in the folklore of the county. Harding's daughter had her father's red-plush waistcoat altered to fit her and wore it to the end of her life to exhibit the bullet hole that her father survived at the deciding fight with the Dunsdons, bringing curious travellers to the remote Bird in Hand Inn.

A century earlier, across the Cotswolds, where rolling wolds give way to sweeping commons, the Ragged Cot by Minchinhampton had an equally dramatic story unfolding within its old stone walls. Bill Clavers led the double life of innkeeper and highwayman in 1660. Despite the fact that his young wife had fallen down the stairs with their baby in her arms in a desperate attempt to stop him going out on yet another mission, loaded with pistols and too much rum Clavers continued on his mission, and returned home to find them both lying dead where they had fallen. Bundling their bodies into a heavy trunk, Clavers was halted in his effort to hide it away by the constables of the day demanding that he open up in the name of the law. His footprints in the snow had led them from the robbed mail coach to the inn and, attempting to enter by way of a window, the constables were fired upon. The landlord's terrified scream from behind the bolted door puzzled the officers as they had had no time to return fire. They entered with no further resistance from Clavers and roped him to a chair while they searched the premises for proof that he was the highway robber. It was then the turn of the constables to take fright and they fled the inn when faced with the spectral figures of Mrs Clavers and child sitting on the trunk. Clavers was released the next morning in daylight and explained that he had been startled by the sight of his wife and child rising from the trunk. The bodies were found inside the bound trunk and Clavers was duly dispatched for their murder. Earlier this century, ghostly noises and footsteps returned to the inn for a period. A comment in the visitors' book, by one of the American servicemen

The Ragged Cot, Minchinhampton.

who made what they termed 'The Jagged Pot' their local during the last war, reads 'It is three miles to the Cot, but nine miles back'!

It is the ghost of a former landlady who drowned in the River Coln, on which The Mill Inn stands, that is reputed to be one a number of spirits attributed to the lovely old inn at Withington. It is a young child's patter of footsteps that run on occasion through the upstairs rooms at The Corner Cupboard at Winchcombe. Built as a farmhouse around 1550 it became an inn in 1872 and took its name from the extraordinary number of corner cupboards found there.

Moreton-in-Marsh is reckoned to be a ghost hunter's Mecca; the Manor House Hotel claims to be the most haunted building in the town, with the ghost of Dame Creswyke being the most frequently identified, returning to the former family home where she was murdered three centuries ago. Poltergeists, a phantom pipe smoker and a man paddling his feet in the horse pond are numbered among Moreton's many spirited visitors, with the White Hart adding the spectre of a Cavalier, seen on occasion in its bar.

This is Civil War country, and Stow-on-the-Wold has its own special Royalist. A *Guinness Book of Records* contender as the 'Oldest Inn in England', The Royalist Hotel in Digbeth Street dates back to AD 949, when it was a leper hospice; the remainder of a leper hole through which the afflicted outcasts received their meagre daily bread still exists in the oldest part of the hotel. I asked one of the friendly waitresses about its ghost. 'Which one?' she queried. There are a couple of Victorian-dressed children, a regal lady dressed in lace, a black knight and, as might be expected in a place where such an important and bloody battle occurred on its very doorstep, the ghostly Royalist is also listed among the sightings and unexplained sounds. Whether the cavalier is John Shellard, who vanished in the tumultuous Civil War years, or the restless soul of one of the 200 wounded Royalists who were so mercilessly butchered in the town centre, is unknown. Descendants of the Shellard family who owned the building, known as Porch House in the early 1600s (Thomas Shellard's initials can still be seen carved above the front porch he built in 1615), have visited The Royalist, tracing their family connections. They have discovered that a Tom Shellard is recorded as having seen an apparition there in 1960, which he believed to be his long dead ancestor. The faint outline of a young man in high boots, waisted coat and bandoleer seen on the staircase was how Tom Shellard described the apparition, calling the experience 'ominous and spooky'. The matter of young John Shellard's disappearance all those years ago must forever remain a mystery, but the long finger of suspicion has pointed to his own kith and kin, conveniently 'removing' the messenger for the King's cause around Oxford in the age when brother was set against brother, especially as

The Corner Cupboard, Winchcombe.

The Royalist Hotel, Stow-on-the-Wold, England's oldest inn and host to a number of ghostly guests.

A Witch Post by the fireplace in the Royalist Hotel.

there was an inheritance at stake. A secret passage that led from the corner of the fireplace in the present bar is said to run underground for nearly a mile to Maugersbury Manor. It is feasible that the young John might have used this as an escape route when Cromwell's troops were too close for comfort. During the Second World War a passage was found leading from the hotel cellar – I was allowed to go down to see for myself, and although the end had been bricked up for many years and racks of wine filled the centre, I found the atmosphere to be one of palpable mystery trapped in that ancient circular walled chamber.

Witches and their supernatural powers were as feared as if they were armed soldiers, and the custom of warding them off by making a 'witch mark' in the stone fireplace is one of great antiquity. Entrances to houses were protected by supernatural deterrents, such as a horseshoe on the doorpost (witches are supposed to hate iron) and secretive signs incised on a fireplace, to prevent them slipping down the chimney and taking the household unawares. For good measure, the Royalist has a witch post, made of Rowan wood (a traditional deterrent) next to its impressive witch mark in the dining room. The Tudor stone fireplace had been hidden for centuries until the 1970s renovation work at the hotel revealed its secrets and, though time has blurred the detail, it is still possible to trace the outline of some of the symbols making up the witch's mark.

The Fleece Inn at Bretforton, voted CAMRA's Pub of the Millennium, is caught in a timber and whitewash time warp. There has been no covering up of its witch mark. In fact, in this pub there is no quarter given to fickle fashion at all – neither in furnishings nor food fads. The legendary Lola Taplin, late hostess of The Fleece, saw to it that nothing would ever change here, by willing it to the National Trust with strict conditions attached as to its continuity. The Fleece is the only one of the National Trust's three dozen Cotswold pubs and inns that cannot sell the ubiquitous packets of crisps. Lola did not like them. Lola also did not like any of her prized pewter platters going missing during the Second World War, and let it be known to the Commander of the nearby American base that The Fleece would be out of bounds to the servicemen until the pewter was returned. The officer's persuasive powers were obviously strengthened by the fact that it was well known to be his favourite watering hole! Lola may be gone from her little earthly paradise as she died in 1984 but she is not gone in spirit, according to local folk – her distinctive old-fashioned lavender perfume still wafts through the four-teenth-century inn on occasion.

This is Shakespeare's Cotswold country, so it is not surprising that one of the tourist attractions of his home town is a 'Stratford Ghost Tour'. It is all too easy to consign tales of the unexpected to the distant past, to be recounted on a winter's night by the warm glow of the fire's dying embers, when one is earth-bound in the depths of a favourite armchair with a half-finished glass of cheer. But, to finish this chapter, here is another story: a former pilot with the Red Arrows aerobatic team was convinced that it was the guiding spirit of a wartime pilot, who had crashed near the team's former training base at Kemble, that saved his life some thirty years later. The local newspapers ran the story of how Flt Lt Lloyd Grose, who was Red 5 in the Red Arrows 1978 team, was horrified to realise he was about to hit Kemble Wood at well over 200 knots in his Gnat jet. He describes the following: 'by the time my brain had alerted my senses to pull back on the control column, to my utter amazement, and quite unaccountably, I found myself skimming the treetops before the aircraft had started to climb. I am convinced that a greater being came to my rescue. Thank you, Twinkle.' Twinkle was the nickname given to Flt Lt Ronald Pearson (the name arose from his characteristic walk) whose Hurricane crashed into the woods in 1943. Decorated with the Distinguished Flying Cross, the thirty-year-old pilot was buried at All Saint's church, but his ghost has been reported as returning to the former airfield within the last decade.

5
MYSTERIES & LEGENDS

The Rollright Stones, the region's most imposing monument of pre-history, could well be christened Cotswold's Stonehenge, but for the fact that the closer one gets to them the more they assume a very unique form, character and grouping. Antiquarians date this monolithic mystery as pre-Stonehenge. Locked in local legend, the stony tableau is said to be a petrified army of long ago who, under the leadership of Rollandri (Roland the Brave), the Champion of Christianity, set out to conquer all England. As they got to the top of the windswept hill in the north-east Cotswolds, a witch suddenly appeared and promised the would-be conqueror:

> *If Long Compton thou canst see*
> *Then King of all England thou shalt be*

Roland, inspired by such prediction, cried:

> *Stick, stock, stone*
> *As King of England I shall be known.*

He took the obligatory seven strides forward but there in front of him arose a great ridge, blocking the view to the village below. 'Ah, ha', cackled the old witch:

> *As Long Compton thou canst no see*
> *King of all England thou shalt not be*
> *Thou and thy men hoar stones shalt be*
> *And I shall be an elder-tree.*

And that is what they all became. The great circle, measuring some 100ft across and consisting of a reputed twenty-seven stones – the exact number defies accurate counting as it is reckoned no-one gets the same figure twice – are the soldiers. A little way off there is another small group, the Whispering Knights, caught in a conspiratorial huddle as they plotted treason against their leader. And all alone, and actually in the next county – as all this took place on the Oxfordshire/Warwickshire border long before administrators drew lines on maps to create separate shires – is poor old Roland. Folklore accorded him the title that in his legendary lifetime he never claimed, for there he stands, melancholic but majestic, as the King Stone.

Besoms, rather than birch brooms, were more associated with Long Compton at one time as it reputedly had more witches than any other place in the Cotswolds.

The Rollright Stones, locked in mystery and legend.

The witch-elder watches over the results of her spell, and for years there was a tradition wherein a curious crowd would gather to witness the midsummer magic when the elder tree was in blossom; they hoped to see it bleed as a cut was made in a branch and to watch the 'King move his head'. Apparently this story is very close to a number of French legends. Long Compton was once reputed to have enough witches living there 'to draw a load of hay up Long Compton Hill'. The belief in witchcraft lingered longer in this area than it did in most others, according to one report of 1875 in which 'a single crazed man, James of Long Compton, assaulted an old woman of eighty, believing her to be a witch'. He also claimed there were sixteen more witches in the village, one of which was supposed 'to ride up the old road in a cheese kibber'. Fairies supposedly dance round the King Stone at night and, like many a standing stone, the King and his Knights are said to walk down the hill at certain times to drink from the spring in Little Rollright Spinney, after which they turn back into men again, join hands and dance around in a circle before returning to take up their mysterious stony stance on the skyline once more. In an 1859 report it was said that 'people from Wales kept chipping bits of stone from the King-stone to keep the Devil off, quoting a man who was offered a pound for a chip at Faringdon Fair'.

The Devil it is!

The Devil's hand is attributed to being behind a number of mysteries that over time have given rise to local legend. Painswick is famous for its churchyard having ninety-nine yew trees, all immaculately clipped and cared for as an impressive setting for its fine church. It has long been the belief that the hundredth yew will not survive, despite the many attempts to replace it, because the Devil kills it off. Like the stones in the Rollright Circle, the actual number of yew trees in the churchyard has defeated the most careful counter – it seems impossible to get the same figure twice! The truth lies, of course, in the fact that some trees have grown together, thus creating their own puzzle through close propagation.

Cam Long Down and Cam Peak are westerly 'outliers', separated from the Cotswold massif many millennia ago, but the geological reason for the Peak being formed is not nearly as exciting as that of local legend. Tradition has it that 'Old Nick' was so piqued at the great number of churches around the region that he planned to dam off the Severn in the Vale below and drown the godly folk therein. With a devil-sized wheelbarrow filled with good Cotswold earth, Old Nick laboured on in the heat of the day, hell-bent on his purpose, but could not find the river. A cobbler chanced across his way, hung all around with shoes and boots

Painswick, famous for its legendary ninety-nine yew trees and fine collection of tombstones.

that he had collected for repair. 'How far is it to the Severn?' enquired the Devil. The cobbler, sensing the stranger was up to no good with such an unearthly load, told him it was such a long and difficult journey that he had worn out all the shoes and boots that he was carrying walking from there. Old Nick changed his mind at such a daunting task and hastily tipped out the load of earth where he stood and skulked back to his nether regions.

As Sure as God's in Gloucestershire

'As sure as God's in Gloucestershire' is one of our oldest sayings, and it is thought to have originated from the extraordinary number of religious houses in the county. Another school of thought is that it stems from the time when Hailes Abbey near Winchcombe housed part of a relic of the Holy Blood. The Abbey was founded by Richard, younger brother of Henry III, in 1246 as a thanksgiving on surviving a disastrous shipwreck off the Isles of Scilly. Richard, who was later crowned King of the Romans, endowed his abbey with liberal magnificence; its splendour and fame was further enhanced when his son, Edmund, brought to it in 1270 the phial of blood, authenticated by Pope Urban IV as Christ's Blood. Displayed in a purpose-built shrine, the holy relic drew pilgrims from far and wide and Chaucer made reference to it in *The Pardoner's Tale*: 'By the blode of Christ that is in Hayles'. Henry VIII went into one of his famous Tudor tantrums on realising that he had been duped into going on pilgrimage to Hailes, paying homage and a few pence to gain absolution from his sins in the sight of the Holy Grail. On examination, the blood was found to be, reputedly, that of a duck! It was little wonder that Hailes was high on the hit list for dissolution. Romantic in ruin, it must have been magnificent in its prime. Stripped of its former glory and grandeur, this one-time Mecca of pilgrimage and the centre of Cistercian Brotherhood, stands now in the silence of skeletal stone. The humble little church close by, built in or around 1130, still stands and shows in its ancient walls a few heraldic symbols of the King of the Romans, who built the great abbey that once overshadowed it.

Prinknash had been an abbatial manor of Gloucester for centuries before the Dissolution. A close examination of associated dates reveals that the story of the last Abbot of Gloucester dying of grief at the suppression of the monasteries was only a pious legend. Gloucester Abbey was surrendered on 2 January 1540 by the Prior and monks under the conventual seal. The Abbey church was elevated to the status of a cathedral, with the Abbot of Tewkesbury made into the first Bishop of

Book of Hailes.

Opposite: *Prinknash, with the bells outside still waiting for their tower.*

Gloucester when the King created the county of Gloucestershire into an Episcopal See. The manor of Prinknash was then rented by Sir Anthony Kingston from the Crown on condition that he preserve forty deer annually for the King's use. For the next three centuries Prinknash was home to a number of famous families of the shire. The most extensive alterations to the estate were made by Thomas Dyer Edwardes who, on becoming a Catholic in 1924, invited the Benedictines of Caldey to make a foundation at Prinknash Park. Four years later six of the monks arrived at Prinknash to convert the manor house into a monastery. As they had left the island, their boat had passed under the arc of a rainbow and, as they were religious rather than superstitious, the monks took it to be a sign of good fortune. Outgrowing the ancient manor house, the Brothers laid the foundation stone for a new abbey in 1939. Over a thousand tons of concrete were put into the foundations; the Second World War halted all building, but in 1972 the monks moved into the abbey they had built themselves. Architecturally light years away from the typical Cotswold grange they had so lovingly repaired – as caricatured in a splendid painting by W. Heath Robinson – Prinknash Abbey catches the light on its stark lines clad in golden Guiting stone to become a modern legend in its own right.

'By comparison with the beautiful traditional manor house, where I spent my first twenty-three years here, this is a ghastly-looking building, but it is functional', said Father Charles Watson. An organ builder and

musician by profession, Father Charles built the abbey's first organ to replace the French harmonium which had previously accompanied the Chant. Like the abbey bells, which are still awaiting their belfry, the organ was built before the building was ready for its installation, so for its first year Father Charles's organ made its music in Gloucester Cathedral, used in many services, performing in the *Messiah* and featuring on several broadcasts. In the organ case are two carvings, the coats of arms of Prinknash and the last Benedictine Abbey of Gloucester, a symbolic link across the schisms of time and religious politics.

The first organ to be built in England is credited to St Adhelm, when he was first Abbot of Malmesbury. Adhelm, celebrated across Europe for his writings, sounds a lively character 'wowing' and 'converting the townsfolk in the old streets with jokes and music'. His prototype organ is quoted as being 'a mighty instrument with innumerable tones, blown with bellows, and enclosed in a gilded case'. St Adhelm's Well, where the Benedictine monk meditated, is legendary for maintaining its depth and temperature all year round, some 60 feet above river level! The river and monastic fish ponds are but one part of the amazing Abbey House gardens, which Ian and Barbara Pollard have restored to encompass the huge history of this site, the final resting place of Athelstan, first King of All England. Their ambitious vision has materialised in what is a visual feast of flora and fauna, history and tranquillity, capturing the very essence of the monastic legacy of learned husbandry, combined with hands-on hard work, attracting awesome accolades from press and visitors alike.

Legends linger long in this part of the world – Malmesbury Abbey gardens are firmly re-established due to the Pollards' outstanding achievement – but Elmer the Flying Monk of Malmesbury has maintained his place in folklore history for a spectacular failure to achieve his ambition. What a stir Elmer must have created a millennium ago, when he revealed his passion for aeronautics; even more so when he strapped a glider-like contraption to himself and 'flew' from the abbey's west tower, monk's habit billowing in the wind. Undeterred by the breaking of both legs and despite being 'lame ever after', Elmer decided that his flying machine would perform better with a tail – but the Abbot banned a second attempt and Elmer turned his attention to studying astronomy.

Winchcombe, like Malmesbury, houses stone coffins from ancient times. Winchcombe lost its abbey in the Dissolution, so it is at the parish church of St Peter's that the relics are on show. The two coffins are those of King Kenulf and his son, Kenelm, who succeeded to the throne of Mercia as a young child. The idea that the young boy king was killed at the instigation of his jealous, older sister, Kendrida, grew from the writings of Richard of Cirencester in the fourteenth century. Chaucer used it in part in the *Nun Priest's Tale*. The tale is full of murderous detail of how the young Kenelm died. But it is the almost scriptural method by which the news appeared on a scroll, taken by a dove to Rome to be deposited on the high altar of St Peter's, with the words: *In Clent cow-pasture under a thorn, Of head bereft lies Kenelm, King born*, and the 'guiding light' by which the search party found the boy's body, that takes it into the realms of incredulity. The drama deepens as the wicked sister's eyes drop out as she publicly proclaims her innocence in the murder, and springs miraculously gush forth from the ground where the body of the boy king was rested as the monks carried him home.

Round Hill spring, which supplies Sudeley Castle, is one of the reputed miracle springs and was called St Kenelm's Well after the young murder victim achieved martyr status. Sceptics attribute the legend to the fabrication of the Winchcombe monks in order to attract some of the pilgrim trade passing on to neighbouring Hailes.

Another St Kenelm's Well in a field at Sapperton also purports to originate from the appearance of the miraculous spring, as a result of the boy king's cortege resting there – but the spot seems unlikely to be connected with the legend unless a very roundabout route was undertaken. The village church there is dedicated to St Kenelm, but so are the ones at Alderley and Minster Lovell.

Minster Lovell also has its own legends. The church and the old manor house, fronted by the winding waters of the Windrush, together make a striking group, but it is the ruinous manor house that holds centre stage, indeed it makes such a dramatic statement in stone that one feels that there must be a legend within its jagged frame – nor does it disappoint, for there are two. Both are tragic tales. The oldest story dates back to medieval times and is given credence in a letter written in 1737 by William Cowper, clerk of the Parliament, to Francis Peck, in his day a reputable antiquary:

> Apropos to this, on the 6 May, 1728, the present Duke of Rutland related in my hearing that, about twenty years then before (viz in 1708, upon occasion of new laying [building] a chimney at Minster Lovell), there was discovered a large vault or room underground, in which was the entire skeleton of a man, as having been sitting at a table, which was before him, with a book, paper, pen, etc., etc.; in another part of the room lay a cap; all much mouldred and decayed. Which the family and others judged to be this Lord Lovell, whose exit hath hitherto been so uncertain.

The Lord Lovell whose disappearance had 'been so uncertain' was Francis, the ninth baron, created Viscount Lovell in 1483 by Richard III for his staunch support of the Yorkist cause. Francis Lovell held the offices of Constable of Wallingford Castle, Chamberlain of the Household and Chief Butler of England – a powerful figure who escaped from Bosworth Field to take part later in Lambert Simnel's rebellion. Reports of his death at the battle of Stoke in 1487 were disputed according to Francis Bacon:

> there went a report that he fled, and swam over Trent on horseback but could not recover the other side . . . and so was drowned . . . But another report leaves him not there, but that he lived long after in a cave or vault.

Bacon's report of a vault seems to be the answer to where the fugitive Lord Lovell fled. The general belief is that he was kept in hiding in the secret room in his old manor house, looked after by a trusty servant who met with some untimely end, leaving his master trapped to starve to death.

The second tragedy has been immortalised in the folk ballad of 'The Mistletoe Bough' by Thomas Haynes Bayly (1797-1839), telling of the young Lovell's bride who disappeared during a Christmastide game of hide-and-seek:

Minster Lovell Hall holds two tragic tales in its romantic ruins beside the Windrush.

> *In the highest – and lowest – the loneliest spot,*
> *Young Lovell sought wildly – but found her not.*
> *And years flew by, and their grief at last*
> *Was told as a sorrowful tale long past…*
> *At length an oak chest, that had long lain hid,*
> *Was found in the castle – they raised the lid*
> *And a skeleton form lay mouldering there,*
> *In the bridal wreath of that lady fair!*
> *Oh! Sad was her fate – in sportive jest*
> *She hid from her lord in the old oak chest.*
> *It closed with a spring – and, dreadful doom,*
> *The bride lay clasp'd in her living tomb.*

The Secret Marriage at Snowshill Manor

Snowshill Manor is steeped in history and mystery. Now owned by the National Trust, the traditional style of the old house, the main part of which dates back to around 1500, belies the curious and varied collection within. The collection is unique – an assemblage of articles and artefacts of such diversity that Queen Mary remarked that the most extraordinary thing about it was the collector. Charles Paget Wade, architect, artist and craftsman, spent his considerable West Indies sugar plantation inheritance, and half a century of his life, arranging and restoring the house and gardens in which to exhibit his eclectic collection. Curious character as he was himself, Charles Wade uncovered a clandestine romantic mystery in his own house to equal any novelist's invention. His account of how it all began is dated 1953 – some three years before his death:

> When repairing the ceiling of this room I sent a fragment of one of the beams to a lady in Brighton, who, I was told, had a remarkable gift of seeing into the past and future. (She would not accept any fees, and was not a professional 'seer'). She had never heard of Snowshill, but described it as if she were there:
>
> 'Two houses set upon a steep slope, the larger – lofty and mysterious, the other smaller and homely. In the larger house – an upper room – it's late at night, in it a girl in a green dress of the seventeenth century, much agitated, paces up and down. She does not live there, and will not stay the night.'
>
> This seems a pointless tale without beginning or end. However, some years later, Mrs Clegg lent me some papers relating to Wormington Grange by E.A.B. Barnard, FSA, F. Hist. Soc., in which were details of the Star Chamber case relating to the secret marriage of Ann Parsons.
>
> Charles Paget Wade, 1953

Snowshill – the scene of a seventeenth-century secret marriage of which the church knew nothing.

Ann Parsons, who was fifteen years of age at the time of these events, came from the Parsons family of Overbury. Both her parents had died and Ann's mother, Goodithe Parsons, who later had lived at Wormington, had made a will in 1602, in which the greater part of an estate valued at 1,000 marks would go to Ann at the age of sixteen, or on her marriage. The guardianship and tuition of the young heiress was in the hands of Richard Daston, half brother to and co-executor with Sir William Savage of Elmley Castle. A marriage contract was drawn up between Ann and George Savage, Sir William's youngest son, before George took up an apprenticeship in London. While George was away a servant in the Savage household, Anthony Palmer, carried on a clandestine courtship with Ann Parson, persuading her that he would be a better match for her than Sir William's son and promising to bestow on the young heiress a house and lands.

On Valentine's Eve 1604 Ann was abducted from Sir William's house by Anthony Palmer and a number of companions, using armed force to enter, and forcibly carrying Ann away. They first went to Broadway, home village of the Palmer family, and then on to Snowshill, to be joined at the manor by the Revd Richard Stone, vicar of St Eadburg's church. In an upper room of the medieval great hall, at the stroke of midnight, a marriage ceremony was performed, 'contrary to the Laws of God and the Church'. The owner of Snowshill Manor at the time was John Warren, whose brother Richard had married Jane Parsons of Overbury. But, true to the sense of the past felt by Charles Wade's correspondent, Ann was unwilling to spend the night in the manor house, and went with her bridegroom to Chipping Campden.

Sir William and a band of servants pursued the newly-weds, and regained possession of his recalcitrant charge, placing her under the care of her grandmother, Ann Lagston, an aged gentlewoman living at Sedgeberrow. On discovering the hiding place of his new bride, Anthony Palmer, again with his confederates, used considerable force to take her from the house, beating the old lady and 'thrust through her right hand with a dagger'. In due course all the participants in the plot were charged with the abduction of Ann Parsons, contriving the unlawful marriage between her and Anthony Palmer 'when she had been solemnly contracted and betrothed to George Savage', and a second attempted abduction at Sedgebarrow. The defendants swore that they 'ought not to answer since the circumstances of the marriage were spiritual matters determinable in an ecclesiastical court'. A Commissioner of Peace was eventually appointed and depositions of witnesses were taken at Evesham on 17 January 1605.

Among the deponents was Anthony's sister, who denied that any abduction had taken place, saying that on St Valentine's Eve, Ann

Parsons '*did goe from the house of complainante to meete*' Anthony Palmer and that she (Anne Palmer) was unaware of the alleged contract of marriage. She was accused of being the ringleader of the plot, taking advantage of Ann Parson 'being a simple girle, disabled and dispraised' the life she would lead if she married George Savage, tempting her with a '*convenyent house and lands to the value of fourscore pounds per annum*' (in the full knowledge that her brother never had, and was most unlikely to, own any property). Richard Stone, the Broadway cleric who performed the secret marriage ceremony at Snowshill Manor, swore that '*he doth not knowe the said George Savage, but doth know the said Ann Parsons and hath seene her twyse*'. It would seem that the vicar had been an unwitting party to the set-up, ignorant of the former betrothal and perhaps believing the Palmer family, who were respected locally, to be swayed by romance rather than religion in the chosen venue for the marriage. Stone is reported as giving but a brief reply in answer to his involvement in the plot, avoiding any reference to the ceremony. There is no record of the marriage, secret or otherwise, either in the Snowshill or Stanton Registers.

The secret marriage remains a mystery – that it happened is borne out by the Star Chamber Proceedings, James I, 1604. Whether by abduction or agreement, whether the jilted George received compensation for losing his betrothed heiress, or even whether Ann and Anthony lived together happily ever after is not known. But there is a tantalising tailpiece to the story, because after Ann died she is recorded in 1682 by the Heralds in their Visitation to Worcestershire as 'Ann Clarke of the pedigree Parsons of Overbury'. When did husband Clarke appear in Ann's life?

The legendary love tale lives on – the room where the secret marriage took place was named by Charles Wade as Ann's Room. The inscription over the door translates to *You Cannot Conceal Love or a Cough*.

How much married were they?

At the other end of the social scale is the 'Half Marriage' at Horsley. This was conducted in the village church, and it is recorded. In 1732 the vicar wrote:

> John Pegler and Ann Thomas were half married August 11. I proceeded no further because they paid me but one half 2s 6d.

The mystery here must be which half was married? How married were they exactly, and how legal is a half marriage?

Chipping Campden holds its 'Wonder' place in the history of mysteries.

The Campden Wonder

The wonder about this tale is in its power to still excite the imagination of writers and test the logic of the learned of today – some three and a half centuries after the event happened. The story of the Campden Wonder, as the mystery is popularly known, is a historical whodunit of legendary proportions. A ballad published in London in 1662 gave a contemporary view in 'Truth brought to Light, or Wonderful and True News from Gloucestershire'. But it is the truth that has evaded those who have examined the story in detail, to become one of the most puzzling mysteries in English history.

In 1660 William Harrison, steward to Lady Juliana Noel of Chipping Campden, disappeared after collecting her Ladyship's rents. He was last reported seen going about his duty in Charingworth on 16 August, where he had collected the equivalent of £23. A search for the missing steward produced no body, but a battered hat, a bloodstained collar and a comb was found by John Perry, servant to William Harrison. Suspicion fell on Perry and, no doubt after a deal of distressing interrogation, he confessed to his master's murder, aided by his brother, Richard, and their mother, Joan, who was reputed to be a witch. Despite the mother and brother protesting their complete innocence, and John Perry changing his story at the last minute about murdering William Harrison, and despite there being no body to back up the charge against them, the three were hanged on Campden Hill. Two years later, William Harrison 'walked back into Campden'.

His story, accounting for his two years' disappearance, was so dramatic as to range into the realms of romantic fantasy, and it is this that has been the enduring mystery. Harrison purported to have been attacked and abducted by three horsemen near Ebrington, taken to Deal and put on a ship bound for the American slave market, but the ship with its miserable human cargo was seized by Turkish pirates and the Cotswold man ended up in North Africa instead. There he was sold as a slave to 'an aged physician of Smyrna'. Harrison was already a relatively elderly man, but was reputed to have a wide knowledge of herbs. When the old physician died he left his English worker a silver gilt drinking bowl. Freed from his captive service, Harrison sold the bowl to help pay for his passage home and returned to his post as steward at Court House, where he must have regained local respect as reports speak of him serving as a trustee of Campden Grammar School.

The former Campden House had been razed some fifteen years before all this happened, apparently on the orders of Prince Rupert, to prevent it falling into Parliamentary hands. Historians believe that Harrison, as

Lady Juliana Noel, a key figure in the dramatic tale of the Campden Wonder.

steward in charge of the mansion, was a man who knew too much. When Charles II was restored to the monarchy and investigated the burning down of certain properties it is thought that his nephew, Prince Rupert, Colonel Henry Bard, the Royalist officer occupying Campden House at the time of the destruction, and the Noel family (conveniently absent at the time) had good reason for getting Harrison out of the way for a while until the investigations were over. It is feasible that the hapless 'simple-minded' John Perry (whom some believe to have been Harrison's illegitimate son) was party to a plot that went horribly wrong. He paid the price with his own life and the sacrifice of his brother and mother in the most bizarre case of a miscarriage of justice for a murder that never was. It is not so much a whodunit as who did what, and what did they all really do and why!

Violence on St Valentine's Day, 1945

There certainly was a body present in this next tale, one of the most baffling cases of murder that brought Scotland Yard to the Cotswolds, and there was absolutely no doubt from the state of the body that it was murder. But proving who did it and why has proved impossible, leaving the case as one of the rare few still open in the Yard's files to this day. The victim, seventy-four-year-old Charles Walton, was one of those enigmatic country characters that could have stepped out of the pages of a Thomas Hardy novel, a man of the soil, half crippled with rheumatism, wise in the ways of wild animals and birds of hedgerow and field in Lower Quinton, his lifelong home, but reticent with most of his fellows, traditionally preferring to drink at home than with his neighbours in the nearby pubs, the Gay Dog and the College Arms. Following the death of his wife, Walton lived with his niece, Edith Walton, in the middle cottage of a storybook black and white thatched terrace.

When Charles Walton failed to return home by the time darkness fell on 14 February 1945 after a day hedge-cutting at The Firs farm, Edith called on her neighbour to help her search for her uncle, fearful that he had been taken ill or met with an accident. Alfred Potter, the farmer for whom the old hedger was working on the slopes of Meon Hill, joined in the search. Finding Walton by the light of a torch, pinned to the ground by his pitchfork and his throat slashed in a form of a cross, made grisly reading in the newspapers and the bizarre base for the ensuing lengthy investigations, suspicions, whispers of witchcraft and sacrificial ritual in ancient fertility rites. The famed Fabian of the Yard, a famous inspector, joined forces with the Warwickshire CID and the case took on monumental status. One theory had been that the method of killing was so

One of the picture-postcard cottages at Lower Quinton that was home to the mysterious and ill-fated Charles Walton.

brutal and ritualistic that it was 'un-English', and every one of the 1,043 prisoners-of-war in the nearby camp at Long Marston was closely interrogated. Of mixed nationality – Italian, German, Ukranian and Slav – the only prisoner among them found to be a likely suspect was an Italian who had bloodstains on his coat; a laboratory test proved it was rabbit's blood from a crafty bit of poaching for supper. A squad from the Royal Engineers scoured the woods and fields around with metal-detectors, searching for clues and the old man's watch that was missing off its chain on his coat; every soul in the villages of Lower and Upper Quinton and Admington was interviewed.

The mystery of the old man's murder extended to reflections on the mystery of the old man himself; his tin watch, which bore a Stratford-upon-Avon jeweller's name, was discovered some years later and found to contain a black glass. Speculation that it was a 'witch's glass' raised again the supernatural spectre that had haunted the case from the beginning. His uncanny affinity with creatures of fur and feather, with an extraordinary ability to commune with and direct them to follow his commands, were later considered to be unnatural. Alfred Potter, who from his evidence was the last one to see Walton alive, changed his story about the time he had seen the old man, and even cast doubts as to whether it was Walton after all. His fingerprints were on the pitchfork – but he was

productive of great sport. His Royal Highness, The Prince of Wales was present during the four days.'

Trainers and riders centred on the area and when Dangerous, owned and trained by William Sadler at Aldsworth and ridden by F. Chapple, won the Derby in 1833, a look-out was posted on the church tower to watch for its return to the village. At the given news, the Sunday service was suspended – with the agreement of the vicar – so that the victorious horse, trainer and rider could be given an appropriate welcome home.

A darker side of the racing legend of the Bibury Races is said to be within the walled enclosure of 'Sadler's Clump'; the gaunt metal pylons of our modern age have now replaced the trees that once marked the spot, named after the notable trainer, who counted the 1830 as well as the 1833 Derby winners among his string of successes. It is here, legend has it, that the truth behind the Running Rein scandal lies buried. The three-year-old Running Rein was entered for the Derby, but a 'ringer' – a four-year-old named Maccabeus – ran in its place and won, to be

Jockey Club plaque in the Sherborne Arms at Aldsworth, a reminder of the heady days of Bibury Races held in the parish until 1849.

shot immediately after the race and buried under 'The Clump' to avoid investigation. But the fraud was uncovered by Sir George Bentinck, and the placings officially re-arranged with the horse called Orlando awarded as the true winner.

Among the old race meetings memorabilia on the walls of the Sherborne Arms, a village pub proper and the second to bear the name in Aldsworth, are a couple of circular plaques commemorating the bicentenary of the Derby with all the Derby winners on – including those from the small Cotswold village itself. The Enclosure Map of 1799 shows the first inn to bear Lord Sherborne's arms was at the entrance to the village off the main road. *The Oxford Journal* advertising the races to be held for the Burford Cup in 1797, stated that all the runners would be shown at the Sherborne Arms on the day before the races began. Jockey stables were marked on the map as being next to the inn.

The first Sherborne Arms closed in 1845, and a house was built on the site. The vicar of the day, the Reverend John Bellingham, claimed the credit for 'abolishing the races, banishing the stable and suppressing the public house' after the royal patronage and presence had gone with the death of the first Lord Sherborne, leaving the races which had before been the forum for the rich and the famous, the noble and the fashionable, to become infamously attractive due to the vast crowds of visitors 'of the lowest and most abandoned description'. The Sabbath had been turned into a day for opening of shops, 'Sunday games and sports and wrestling, boxing, cockfighting and cricketing on the village green… creating considerable disorder and licentiousness among the parishioners'. After a defiant and abortive attempt to reinstate the Bibury Race Club meetings at Aldsworth, the last ever took place on the Seven Down course in 1849. Not only the vicar had cause for complaint for disruption to everyday life in the small Cotswold village: a local farmer got so fed up with race-goers taking a short cut across his field of standing corn he spread red raddle along the route – staining the petticoats and breeches of the offenders!

And a Tale by Moonlight

Perhaps the legend of Moonlight of Tetbury is the appropriate tailpiece here. One of Tetbury's claims to fame is that it seems to have none. Throughout its long history it is a town that has escaped 'incidences' in over a thousand years of national and international turmoil and conflict. The nearest skirmish in the Civil War was on the other side of the ditchhedge that marked the parish boundary. The Second World War brought depots and airfields and factories and army bases all around and the town did suffer a few air raids – but the only casualty was Tom Rich's cow. Moonlight was a black cow with a white face, and she was literally blown sky high in one raid, to be found in parts from the top of the town to the council houses – the tale of just how many families dined off Moonlight is locked now in local lore.

6

Curiosities

THE QUAINT & THE CURIOUS

The pinnacle of rock jutting out of the scarp face at Leckhampton, known locally and recorded officially on OS maps as the Devil's Chimney, is the Cotswolds' most famous natural landmark. The old GWR days of intimate, plush upholstered carriages with hammock-style luggage racks, advertised rail trips to Cheltenham Spa with a picture of the Devil's Chimney. Fit and fearless cyclists swarmed to the spot to have their photograph taken against its silhouette, while the totally reckless risked life and limb to climb it, always leaving a coin on its cap as a token to Old Nick, the affectionate term for the Devil, whose monumental work folklore reckons it to be. The record number of people clinging perilously together on the precipitous top stands at thirteen; climbing the Chimney nowadays is strictly prohibited and indeed made impossible by the protective measures undertaken a decade ago to save it from collapse. Erosion of the much loved and enigmatic landmark and the danger of losing it caused such a passionate response from the public that it was repaired for a heftier sum than any mortal would expend on their chimney, and it was conserved as part of our Cotswold heritage.

The hill on which it stands was bought by Cheltenham District Council in 1929 and is scheduled as a Site of Special Scientific Interest for its natural grasslands that make up the 400-acre common. Just how

The Devil's Chimney at Leckhampton.

the curiously shaped outcrop of rock evolved has exercised the minds of geologists and antiquarians for years. The fact that this pile of stone piled upon stone was described as early as 1803 as 'one of these scars, from its craggy and gigantic form is called the Devil's Chimney' attracts more attention to the origin of its name than that of a geological reason.

Leckhampton hilltop quarries were worked extensively in the eighteenth century to build Georgian Cheltenham in the vale below, and it was here on the highest range of the escarpment that the first Cotswold railway was attempted. Initially worked on a pulley system, the stone was brought down to the main road and empty trucks hauled up. The industrially minded Victorians first used horse-drawn trams, then engine-drawn rail trucks until 1925. Once the track had been cut and the pillar of stone separated from the hillside mass, it is thought that the final capping of the pinnacle was a quarryman's joke – it soon became such a feature that it was reckoned to have been a publicity stunt to attract visitors to the new spa town. This theory is less fanciful perhaps than that proposed by one writer, who suggested it was a folly created by shepherds whiling away a few idle hours while tending their flocks on the hill.

As is their wont, it is the folklorists who came up with the most interesting answer that has stood the test of time. The Devil, determined to wreak revenge for the Church's hold in the Cotswolds, hid among the rocks on the edge of Leckhampton Hill and picked out great lumps of the stone to hurl down on the monks and pilgrims trekking below to the ancient Hailes Abbey. His evil intent backfired as he wrestled with a particularly heavy and deeply embedded rock, the seam split open and an avalanche of stone fell on top of him sending him to the bottom of the hill. He lies now, deep down in the Cotswold limestone below Dead Man's Quarry – the Chimney marking the spot. The Devil's Table, another slab of eroded stone, a little way southwards, echoes the legend again to the long-distance walkers who follow the Cotswold Way route along the escarpment. Despite the tale of Old Nick's demise, fossil hunters often find the 'Devil's toenails' in the Severn clays by Hock Cliff. Our forefathers made good use of them: ground down and mixed with the whey separated from the curds in cheese-making, they made a fine medieval cattle cure-all!

Broadway Tower makes a dramatic punctuation mark on the north-westerly tip of the Cotswolds. Its 65ft castellated turrets dominate the skyline on the second highest point of the region. Designed by James Wyatt for the sixth Earl of Coventry in an age when follies were in fashion, the tower on Broadway Beacon was built in a darker stone than the native limestone to create an appearance of brooding maturity. A rather grandiose gesture in adding to the catalogue of follies built

Broadway Tower.

by wealthy landowners in the eighteenth and nineteenth centuries, Broadway Tower does not fall easily into the usual description of contemporary follies as useless extravaganzas or whimsical edifices, but does have the element of romantic fantasy in its design that is essential in all such architectural 'shams' – as they are so often categorised. It is not in disguise, as so many follies are, or built as a secret trysting spot, as the one at Stancombe Park, where a vicar of North Nibley met his gypsy lover. The romantic Reverend had his folly built in the valley well away from the house, outwitting his well-proportioned spouse who might have been tempted to follow him through the secret garden by having the tunnels leading to it so narrow that she was totally unable to get through them. Broadway Tower stands in splendid isolation on its hill, a solid statement of its purpose as an excellent viewpoint. And this is exactly what it was designed for: the Earl of Coventry had it built in 1799 for his wife who, being so enchanted with the fact that a victory bonfire lit on Broadway Beacon could be seen by the family at Croome Court, Worcester, requested that a tower be built as a landmark and reminder of their Springhill estate. The view from the hilltop is extensive; the view from the top of the tower is panoramic. A record twelve counties can be seen from here – this was thirteen before the county planners drew new pencil lines along old shire boundaries. Extending over a hundred miles in each direction, on a clear day Shropshire's Wrekin can be seen in the

The Lygon Arms, Broadway.

north; beyond Bredon Hill, an outlier of the Cotswolds, and Evesham in its vale, to the Clee and the Clent and the Malverns; east to west from Border Hill of Leicestershire to the Welsh Black Mountains, and southwards to Cleeve Hill, the highest point on the Cotswold escarpment, offering 'the broadest view in all England'. The Earl sold both Broadway Tower and Springhill Estate in around 1830: the former to the eccentric bibliophile Sir Thomas Phillips and the latter to General Lygon. The General's butler kept an astute eye on the strategic position of Broadway village as a staging post for the London to Worcester coaches and bought the sixteenth-century White Hart Inn from his lord and master – who was totally engrossed in planting his Springhill estate with beech trees, emulating the formation of the troops under his command at Waterloo. The butler renamed the inn the Lygon Arms, and displayed the coat of arms in honour of his part in the great victory. The inn became one of the most prestigious hotels in the country, and Broadway a 'must see' village on every tourist's itinerary, although it is William Morris who is credited with having 'discovered' Broadway. It was an artists' enclave. Morris described it as 'heaven on earth' when he stayed there with Burne-Jones and Rossetti – but did complain about the steep climb to it when laden with heavy picnic baskets. The Tower still holds its earlier associations within its walls in the form of a museum, and is the centrepiece of a country park offering a varied range of interests and activities.

Court Leet and a Coat of Arms

Tetbury 'revived' its Court Leet in about 1912 and the present Feoffees still have an active role in the town's affairs, with the Millennium Green at the foot of Gumstool Hill and the growth of Berkeley Wood being more recent projects, as well as administering charitable bequests. The Feoffees present their accounts before a public meeting that takes place after the traditional Beating of the Bounds on or around Michaelmas Day – evidence of their ancient office finding a role in today's civic affairs. But it is the place the two dolphins have in the town's coat of arms that has puzzled the historians. The earliest mention of a seal of the town of Tetbury is dated the feast of St Denis (9 October) 1397; the earliest pictographic reference of the dolphins was found on two trade tokens, one undated, but thought to be of the same date as the one marked 1669, bearing the inscription on the obverse: 'This. Farthing. Will. Be. Owned = In Tetbury'; the next oldest example extant is on a pair of constables' staves preserved in the Town Hall. It is generally thought that the clue lies in the reference in the town's Mercian charter of AD 681 which refers to its role as a trading centre. Yet another theory, and possibly the one most likely to explain why land-locked Tetbury sports a pair of dolphins in its coat of arms, is that they were symbolic of the Berkeley feudal ties until 1633 when the town bought itself from Lord Berkeley for £850. Local historians quote hearsay that 'at one time servants in the Berkeley livery wore collar badges of single dolphins'. Searches by both the College of Arms and the Gloucestershire Records Office throw no more authoritative light on the mystery: in fact, the professional conclusion was 'It is pretty evident that Tetbury has no right to any Coat of Arms and it still remains to discover where the dolphins came from.'

And a Whale of a Tale

The river plays a prominent part in Evesham's history and there are marks on the Northwick Hotel and a large oak tree in the waterfront park opposite giving the height of floods a century ago, but the jaw bones of a whale arching in front of the tree certainly arouses curiosity. A small plaque explains it all:

> The whale was captured by the ship Andrew Marvel in the year 1820 and presented by Mr Stanton, formerly of Evesham (who assisted in the capture) to the late Dr Beale Cooper, in whose grounds near here it stood for upwards of 80 years. Presented in the year 1906 to the Borough by Mrs Frances Edwards, Dr Cooper's grand-daughter.

Well, one wonders what else can one do with such an inheritance – it is hardly something you can tuck in a drawer and forget about! As it happens, it makes an attractive if rather incongruous feature alongside the placid inland river where local anglers fish for smaller fry.

Rough Justice

Ancient feudal control over trading, law and order, education and the welfare of the sick and the poor, lingered on in many places until they became national concerns and parochial council affairs. Despite the wide-ranging benefactions bestowed on Winchcombe by Emma Dent of Sudeley Castle, her influence over the town's matters eventually came to be resented. Intensely interested in the ancient borough's history, she founded a museum at the castle, but the townsfolk insisted that she return the curious seven-holed stocks to them in 1887. The old whipping post for public floggings had long since gone, but the quaint odd-holed stocks had still been used within that generation's memory when in 1860 a man was put in them as a punishment for being drunk. The fearsome wooden

Whale jaw bones at Evesham.

Winchcombe's curious seven-hole stocks.

stocks are preserved outside the International Police Museum, where an attractive tiled roof protects them from the elements – a nicety denied to the unfortunate felons who found themselves clamped in them to suffer what abuse and rubbish their fellows hurled at them. The seven holes design is unique in the Cotswolds and was built to accommodate the local one-legged trouble maker who always managed to get himself 'stocked up' with other miscreants (at least that is what the curator told me!). John Oakley in his memoirs of life in Winchcombe described how he found the stump of the town's ducking stool, which had been used for punishing scolding women and suspected witches, when excavating the foundations for the Vineyard Street bridge, commissioned by Emma Dent to provide a new carriage drive to the castle in 1891.

Unique not only in the Cotswolds, but thought to be unique in the whole of the country, are the 'spectacle stocks' at Painswick. These seventeenth-century leg irons were used as a deterrent within long-lived memory when 'young Mary', who had peculiar powers of healing animals on the strength of being born a 'chime child' (at the stroke of midnight on Good Friday), aroused suspicion about her purported magical prowess. The squire, whose dog Mary had cured so miraculously, intervened and threatened to have the whispering slanderers put in the stocks instead.

Spectacle stocks at Painswick.

Rough justice was certainly rougher in some places than others; in about 1655 Samuel Clift, a clothier of Avening, was beaten up by the churchwardens, put in the stocks at Nailsworth, before being dragged off to Gloucester Gaol 'for standing silent with his hat on in Minchinhampton Church'. Extracts from *Jackson's Oxford Journal 1753-1835* give a vignette of life in those early days:

1775: Assizes cases

Robbery of a woman of one shilling, some halfpence and a metal ring on the King's Highway: Death

Stealing a grey mare: Death

Stealing a hog: Death

Having fished with nets, in the night-time, and on suspicion of killing some fish: To be transported seven years

Stealing two ells of linen cloth: To be branded in the hand and confined for one month (a woman)

Stealing the silver tops of three castors: To be privately whipped

Causing a parish pauper to be committed to Bridewell and there kept on bread and water, till he died through extreme want: Acquitted

1831: On Tuesday last a man, named Mash, was fined 10s and costs for assaulting Mr Wicks, the bell-man while he was going his congratulatory round on Christmas Eve, accompanied by his bell and a copy of verses. The assault was constituted by Mash putting a treacle plaster over the mouth of Mr Wicks.

1834: A master sweep, named Plate, is put in the stocks, as 'obnoxious to peace and good order'.

Quaint and curious was the Act for Burying in Woollen. The wool trade had tumultuous times during the Civil War, and at the Restoration a new stimulus was given to promote woollen cloth sales when a law was passed that every corpse must be buried in wool. An affidavit had to be signed and witnessed certifying that:

(Name) of the Parish (and county) lately deceased, was not put in, wrapt, or wound up or Buried, in any Shirt, Shift, Sheet or Shroud, made or mingled with Flax, Hemp, Silk, Hair, Gold or Silver, or other whatever is made of Sheeps Wooll only, Nor in any Coffin lined or faced with any Cloth, Stuff, or any other thing whatsoever made or mingled with Flax, Hemp, Silk, Hair, Gold or Silver, or any other Material contrary to the late Act of Parliament for Burying in Woollen, but Sheeps Wooll only. (Dated) in the (Year) of the Reign of our Sovereign Lord Charles the Second by the Grace of God, King of England, Scotland, France and Ireland, Defender of the Faith &c, Anno Dom 1684

Entries in old burial registers further testify to the 'buried in wool' law being upheld; evasion, if proven, meant a fine of £5 which was shared between the informant and the poor of the parish. Judging by the scarcity of endorsements in later years the Act was obviously not adhered to for very long and was repealed in 1800.

Writing on the Window and a Painting on the Wall

The haunted inns of the Cotswolds are too numerous to give sufficient story space to, but the Black Horse Inn in Castle Street, built between 1570 and 1600 and believed to be the oldest public house in Cirencester, had not only a ghostly visitation but a ghostly scribe to excite the local press and scare the living daylights out of the landlord's niece in 1933. After Ruby Bower, the niece,

retired to bed about the usual time, no restlessness assailed her and she fell asleep – suddenly, about midnight, she found herself wakeful, uneasy, fearful. Terror overcame her as she opened her eyes and found the room flooded with light. A slight rustling in one corner of the room impelled her gaze in that direction. Her horror increased as she beheld an apparition in the shape of a stout old lady with an evil face and grim expression, gliding slowly across the floor.

The report goes on to say that after the ghostly figure, garbed in a stiff silk fawn-coloured long dress, white apron and frilly mob cap, had disap-

A copy of the curious writing on a window at the Black Horse Inn, Cirencester.

peared through a wall, the light vanished too. Ruby told her uncle and aunt of the incident the next morning and they went with her to the bedroom. 'Nothing unusual met their eyes until they came to the window, and there they found, on a small pane of glass, some old-fashioned hand-writing which was upside down. Mr and Mrs Bower declare this writing was not on the window pane before. It looked as if it had been scratched with a diamond, and was obviously of recent execution. In another room, a pane of glass in the window bears, written in the same handwriting: 'Tom Carpenter John Andrews W 85'. The landlord, when interviewed by a *VWH Gazette* representative, said his niece 'was not a fanciful girl and confessed himself entirely bewildered.'

A close examination of the writing on the window by independent authorities showed the scratches formed part of an attempt to cut a signature into the glass and was obviously new, not having assumed the dark appearance common to cuts made in glass some time previously. The writing, being upside down, was cut from left to right and to the extreme edge of the pane and as far as could be seen, continued behind the lead casing. Yet, it was impossible for a human to cut so near the edge, there being no room for the hand and no space for a cutter or diamond. The words must have been written on a larger sheet of glass, which was then cut to a smaller size, as the lines were seen to naturally flow in a curve off the glass and return in a complete curve to continue the letter, as in the case of the top 'J'. The 'W's' were also curiously formed, both starting with a small square or circle. The landlord and his wife had frequently cleaned the window in the two years they had been at the inn, and both swore that there was no writing on it until the ghostly visit.

A glimpse into a past era gave Peter Juggins, a stone mason of Chedworth, a unique experience. While working on the installation of a display cabinet safe in Cirencester parish church in 1969 to house the famous Anne Boleyn cup, so that it could be viewed by, and at the same time protected from, the general public, Peter describes what happened:

My first task was to draw an opening in the wall, about 2 feet 6 inches square by 2 feet deep. While pulling stones out at arm's length and in semi-darkness, I was surprised to discover parts of an old wall painting. At first I could see only a very small section showing part of a human figure, but gradually other details appeared of what looked like a bonfire, or could it have been a burning bush? By carefully removing more stones I was able to determine part of a bearded face, clouds, a panelled frieze and cherubs blowing like the wind. Most of the colours were very bright as if new, and the main figure was marked with a strong black outline. Just as the whole

Medieval wall painting in Cirencester church, as recalled by Peter Juggins.

scene was revealed, the old powdery plaster disintegrated and the picture shattered into hundreds of tiny fragments. It had obviously been built over for many, many years. However, there were signs that a recess existed at some time as though to view it. I was only able to see this most interesting relic for two or three minutes, but I felt most privileged to have looked on an ancient wall painting that had not been seen by anyone else for many hundreds of years – and humbled that no one can ever see it again. It made such an impression on me and the image imprinted itself on my memory that, although it is now a long time ago since I experienced this vision of the past, I can draw the main features of that wall painting and so record it for posterity.

Daunton's Church of St Mary Magdalene, like Cirencester's Church of St John the Baptist, belonged to the great Augustinian Abbey of Cirencester before the Reformation and, it too, has a fourteenth-century wall painting of major interest. The figure of St Christopher carrying the Child wading through a stream with fishes in green and brown swimming around fills a space some 13 feet high. The wall painting is considerably well preserved. But the tiny Churnside village also has a curious tale told within the pages of its old parish register, as recorded by the minister of the day, Henry Topp:

In this Parish in the Clarke's house, one Richard Syfolly, upon St Matthias Day 1646, about eleven in the forenoon, there rose out of an old dry table-board of birch – on which bord I Henry Topp, Minister here now wright these words August 24th being St Bartholomew's Day – a water, reddish brown of the colour of blood, and so continued this rising an runninge alonge and downe the table, all that afternoon till the next day, and about the hour when it first began, and so it ceased.

No further incidents of this nature have been recorded, but the tale of this curious happening has been handed down the generations and locked in the local folklore.

Reflections on Church Glass

Many a parish church in the Cotswolds has a curiosity within its ancient walls – eccentric and curious clerics aside, there remains many a question to be answered on the fabric of the churches themselves. Within a very small area in the lower Churnside and Coln valleys there are a series of puzzles in the windows alone. It is generally acknowledged that Charles Lutwidge Dodgson, a frequent guest of Canon Henry Liddell, Rector of St Mary's church at Cowley, immortalised the Rector's daughter, Alice, as his *Alice in Wonderland* under the pen of Lewis Carroll. A later whodunit writer might have taken the mysteries of the stained-glass windows in the region as a real world wonder. Starting further down the Churn valley at Siddington there is the question of when St Peter's church will get back its medieval stained glass, taken in around 1800 from the east window of its Langley chapel to be inserted in the great east window of Cirencester church as its central feature – 'on loan'. The terms of the loan were renegotiated in 1867 and according to reports of the time it was promised that the window would be returned to Siddington 'when it could be suitably replaced'. That was nearly a century and a half ago – how long is a loan?

The stained glass of Cirencester's St John the Baptist, the largest parish church in Gloucestershire and one of the most spacious in the kingdom, filled all forty-two windows before the Reformation. Complaints that it was 'not looked after as well as at Fairford', and further damage caused in 1642 when relatives broke some of the windows to get food inside to Prince Rupert's prisoners during the Civil War, resulted in its parlous state by the end of the eighteenth century. The antiquary, Samuel Lysons, undertook the task of having the fragmentary glass collected to go into the great east and west windows (this is obviously the occasion when Siddington's fine medieval glass of the Madonna and Child flanked by

St Catherine and St Dorothy, with the Langley family donors kneeling below, was 'borrowed'). The Cirencester glass that was not re-used was packed into crates and forgotten about, till it was tipped into a ditch at the foot of the railway line at Oakley Hall in around 1890. One case was salvaged but it was not used until 1929 when it was set in the small two-light window above the sedilia in the south sanctuary wall. Even so, the Holy Child of the original fifteenth-century Siddington glass was lost and the present one is by Geoffrey Webb.

Losing irreplaceable medieval stained glass perhaps poses the greatest puzzle and kept the Victorian artists busy with contemporary replacements.

St Mary's at Fairford boasts the only extant complete set of medieval stained-glass windows in the country. Nevertheless, its old 'wool' church still bears the scars of time and the ravages of inclement clime. It was the Great Storm of 1703 that did the most damage and details of its effect at Fairford were written in a letter by the then vicar, the Reverend Edward Shipton, in reply to Daniel Defoe's nationwide survey:

'Honoured Sir, In obedience to your request I have here sent you a particular account... It is the fineness of our church which magnifies our present loss... It is adorned with 28 admired and celebrated windows, which, for the variety and fineness of the painted glass that was in them, do justly attract the eyes of all curious travellers to inspect and behold them... Now that part of it which most of all felt the fury of the winds was a large middle west window, in dimension about 15 foot wide, and 25 foot high, it represents the general judgment, and is so fine a piece of art, that 1500 l. has formerly been bidden for it, a price, though very tempting, yet were the parishioners so just and honest to refuse it. The upper part of this window, just above the place where our Saviour's picture is drawn sitting on a rainbow, and the earth His footstool, is entirely ruined.'

The letter goes on to describe damage caused to other windows on the west side, unbedding sheets of lead on the roof, pinnacles and battlements blown down and then a general assessment of house damage in the town. 'Some of the poor, because their houses were thatched, were the greatest sufferers; but to be particular herein would be very frivolous as well as vexatious.' However, the vicar did think it a prime concern to add that as a result of a thunderstorm on the following day 'a new and strong built house in the middle of our town' had its chimney disjointed, some of the lead of an upper window was melted, and struck the mistress of the house into a swoon – but this proved the effect more of fear, than of any real considerable hurt to be found about her.

It appears that all three west end windows were patched up at once, and evidence from two eminent stained-glass artists in the 1840s showed that much of the Last Judgment glass was retained intact. However, some two decades later there was occasion to have urgent repairs done to the window. During the winter of 1889 Canon Carbonell, who had recently become vicar, and having studied the windows by climbing up ladders and using an eyeglass, found all sorts of anomalies – such as Caiaphas with his legs inside out! Canon Carbonell wrote to the glaziers who had undertaken the earlier repairs and interestingly spoke of 'having accidently heard of pieces of Fairford glass being seen in Birmingham'. Further correspondence in a stronger vein resulted in the return of 'a few small bits they had kept', to which the Canon responded 'There must be many square feet of the old glass somewhere and echo answers where?' Persistent in his pursuit of the missing glass, the Canon then received a letter from Westlake (who had inserted the returned fragments in the two left-hand lights of the south west window) reporting 'that he had seen 12 years ago portions of the west window in Belgium'. A manuscript note of the same period records that 'Samuel Poole of Westminster claims to have one of the heads from the Fairford windows... he made the statement in the hearing of the Clerk of Fairford Church'.

Two questions still await answers: who was it that offered the '1500 *l*' (£1500). for the glass in the early eighteenth century, as quoted by the vicar, Edward Shipton, in his letter to Defoe; and where in Belgium had Westlake 'seen portions of the west window' in what must have been 1878? To know of the artistry and beauty of this treasure in our heritage more than answers the question as to why!

Rose Cottage Transplanted

One of the most controversial, if not curious, historical treasures ever to leave our English shores must surely be that following this advertisement placed in the *Stroud Journal* in January 1929: 'Wanted to purchase, picturesque old world Cotswold cottage. Land optional. Position, history, etc.' H.F. Morton described in his book five years later how he found the ideal cottage:

> ...Then one January day, I chanced to drive through the tiny village of Lower Chedworth which nestles at the bottom of a deep valley between Northleach and Cheltenham, and there I saw 'Rose Cottage'. It had a nice doorway, mullions to the windows, age mellowed drip-stones, and dove holes in the gable. The day was just waning and a cosy light was showing through the old leaded windows, and as everywhere was covered with

Rose Cottage in Lower Chedworth.

Rose Cottage as rebuilt in America.

snow it just looked like a scene on a Christmas card, and I knew that I had found the house I wanted ...

Morton then described how by absolute luck he found the cottage was for sale, visited it the following day and 'was very courteously received by the owner, Mr Smith, and his daughter'. What H.F. Morton did not reveal at the time was that he was being used by his half brother, Sir Percival Perry, to search for a building for Henry Ford, the motor magnate, and Perry's letter to Frank Campsall, Henry Ford's secretary in Dearborn, explained that he 'was taking every possible effort to keep Mr Ford's name from transpiring'. After a great deal of correspondence, plans proposed, amended, accepted and acted upon to 'add any desired features' to 'show the largest number of typical Cotswold features', the renovated and partly rebuilt cottage was taken down. The mason and carpenter involved with the disassembling were to go to Dearborn to supervise the re-erection. The land the buildings stood on was transferred to the Ford Motor Company and sold at a later date. Rose Cottage was in fact two small cottages joined together at their corners, built around the late 1600s, and the barn was used for any additional Cotswold stone needed in the rebuilding.

The stones that made up the cottage were packed in 506 canvas sacks and 211 cases which weighed about 500 tons, filling 68 trucks divided between two trainloads that left the tiny Foss Cross Station, surrounded by an air of impenetrable mystery as it was 'on its way to London Docks and then America'. Every part of the building was numbered and the late Len Hill, 'The Penguin Millionaire', founder of Bourton-on-the-Water's famous Birdland, recalled helping with the restoration, then the dismantling, stone by stone and slate by slate, when he was an apprentice to the Stow-on-the-Wold builder involved in the project:

> My boss said to me 'Laddie, I've got a fortune for you, more than I've ever paid a boy before. Here's 1s 2½d an hour – and £5 from Henry Ford for the work you've done for him'. I'd never had so much money in my life and felt as if I could have bought the street!'

Mr H.J. Gooding of Stow-on-the-Wold, with twenty-seven years experience as a Cotswold 'slatter', according to a report in the *Architects Journal,* became something of a celebrity builder as he worked on building the Cotswold Rose Cottage:

> 'unique in that continent, supervising some seventeen American-born citizens, with two Negroes to roof the house. Souvenir hunters flocked

to the scene of operations for the chance of chipping off bits of genuine Elizabethan tiles from the Old Country'.

Mr C.T. Troughton, a mason, and Mr W.H. Ratcliffe, a carpenter, both Cotswold men, also worked on the reassembling of the old cottage. There had to be some degree of compromise in the actual building: the tiles were put on with copper nails rather than hung on the traditional wooden pegs and a special effort was made to recreate the original texture of the plaster on the walls. According to an interview with a Mr Cutler, an American builder involved in the project at the time, describing the method of mixing wheat chaff with lime plaster:

> they [meaning Cotswold craftsmen] used to put hair in plaster at the time this building was built. This method was learned from the Englishmen who came to supervise the re-erection, and it is a very old method.

A limekiln to Rose Cottage was mentioned in the Will of Joseph Smith, dated 1801, 'And also all that Limekiln and premises which I purchased of John Bridges… and also the bags and other utensils and implements belonging to the said Limekiln'.

The earliest document extant relating to the cottage is an Indenture, dated 1748 between Robert Sley, Mary Sley, Robert and Charles Robins. It then appears to have been through marriage that the Smith family (two of whom are recorded as stone masons) made their home at what was to be eventually called Rose Cottage in Chedworth – now Cotswold Cottage, Henry Ford Museum and Greenfield Village, Michigan.

Henry Ford's passion for uprooting Cotswold buildings, and transplanting them in the United States, was not appeased by acquiring Rose Cottage; his ambitious attempts to remove the whole of Arlington Row from Bibury were, mercifully, stopped. But he did secure an old blacksmith's forge at Snowshill, which had been in the Stanley family for at least three hundred years. It was inspected by Ford and, again, purchased in the name of Morton in 1930. Mr Cox Howman (who altered Rose Cottage to incorporate Ford's 'desired features to be typically Cotswold' – adding, for instance, a more conspicuous dove cote end) was employed to take the forge apart and ship it with all the ironwork to Dearborn, this time 'using a better method of packing – using 100 old beer barrels'. To make the Cotswold scene complete, Ford had a small flock of Cotswold sheep imported to Greenfield Village and a Newfoundland sheep dog named Rover to watch over them and add a living element to the exhibits.

Arlington Row, the early seventeenth-century weavers' cottages at Bibury, was also on Henry Ford's 'souvenir of the Cotswolds' shopping list – but was saved for the nation by the National Trust.

Over 400,000 visitors go to Greenfield Village annually, and 'Cotswold' is a primary source for high school science curricular study, the topic being the heating and cooling of historic buildings. Current renovations to the cottage foundations and roof are being carried out by a stone mason from England. 'Cotswold' is of major importance since the building is older than almost any built in the whole of the United States – giving a unique experience of a seventeenth-century household.

It is a sobering thought that souvenir hunting could have resulted in such a wholesale transportation of a family home; it left much bitterness in its wake back in the Cotswolds, especially in the way the identity of the real buyer and, more importantly, his real intent were kept a closely guarded secret during the sale. The price the great motor magnate paid inflated the price of comparable property, making local people unable to afford to live in the village of their forebears. Henry Ford got his souvenir, it did not simply bear a label saying 'Made in England'; his certificate of authenticity was a Deed dated 1929 (under Morton's name) stating:

Gloucester/Wednesday/April 5, July 5, September 28, November 28, and
Saturday – Horses, cattle, sheep and cheese.

Hampton/Tuesday/Trinity Monday, October 29
The same.

Lechlade/Tuesday/August 10, September 9
The same.

Marshfield/Tuesday/May 24, October 24
The same.

Rudge confined his calendar to market towns stating 'those which are
held in villages are of little importance or use, being consigned to the sale
of pedlary wares'. But fairs were also held in villages, such as Bourton-
on-the-Water, where Mop Fairs were held in May and October. Market
traditions date back to ancient charters, many of which are still extant,
although today's trading bears little resemblance to the mainly livestock
markets of their origin. Many moved from the old towns' central market
places on the coming of the railways to purpose-built complexes with
concrete-based and metal-hurdled pens close to rural stations, from
where large numbers of livestock could be transported in wagons across

*Re-opening Fairford Market in 1986, after it had lapsed as a livestock market following two
world wars, was a festive occasion led by the town's first lady mayor, Mrs Dorothy Paton.*

Minchinhampton Market Hall, built in 1698, was used for entertainments and conducting town business when it ceased its function as a trading centre for wool. Mrs Siddons is said to have played here during the period when she acted at Bath between 1778 and 1782.

Viewed from the church tower, Lechlade Fair spread its attractions all through the main street in 1913.

Daily, daily sing the praises, [with its chorus]
O, that I had wings of Angels
Here to spread and heavenward fly;
I would seek the gates of Sion
Far beyond the starry sky

After the service, the children are presented with a Clipping Bun – a large, extra fruity and spicy bun made especially for the day. A small monetary token is given as well. The other famous Feast speciality of Painswick is the legendary and suspiciously named Puppy Dog Pie. A few years ago I sought the origin of this infamous fare and Peggy Perrin, a true Painswickian, told me the tale told to her by her father, who had it from his grandfather – all this being delightfully reminiscent of the way in which Beatrix Potter heard the tale of the Tailor of Gloucester. The lads of Painswick many years ago had a long-standing feud with their contemporaries of neighbouring Whitehill. Every Saturday night they had their rough and tumble bouts of fighting on the hill, then one night, after the novelty of the weekly scraps had palled, the Painswick boys

Enjoying a Painswick Bun.

called a truce and, as a token of their intent to keep the peace with their neighbours and show hospitality in place of hostility, invited their adversaries to a feast the following week. The Whitehill boys readily accepted and enjoyed the meal of specially prepared meat pies; that is – so the story goes – until their hosts told them they had eaten the dogs of Painswick. For ever after, and even now – but rarely – a local-born man is referred to as a Painswick Bow Wow. It is a tale nurtured over the years and firmly entrenched in the local lore to become a traditional local dish served at family gatherings on Painswick Feast day – the Sunday of the Clipping Ceremony. But the pies are of apple. Peggy Perrin, who kept the local newsagents for years, recalls selling the specially made china pie funnels shaped in the form of a puppy!

Avening Feast is more commonly known as Pig Face Day, from the custom of serving 'pig face' – probably like the boiled then breaded crumbed pig's jowl that we know as Bath Chap. Avening church is dedicated to the Holy Rood, or Cross, and was entirely rebuilt by Queen Matilda, wife of William the Conqueror, in atonement for her revengeful persecution of Brittric, the Saxon Lord of Avening Manor, who rejected her amorous advances when he met her on his earlier ambassadorial mission to Flanders. Matilda then turned 'to her near kinsman' and when William became King of England and she his Queen, she had Brittric thrown into prison and seized his manorial holdings as her own. While the royal couple sojourned at Avening Court, Matilda superintended the building of the church, where Masses for Brittric's soul could be offered. On the consecration on Holy Cross Day, 14 September 1080 (some authorities date it a decade earlier), the Queen gave a feast of boar's head to the builders – and 'pig face' became the main feature of the annual commemorative feast.

Christmas and Easter Feasts, Dumps and Duffs, Dunch and Feggy

> *Stir up we beseech Thee, O Lord,*
> *The wills of thy faithful people*
> *That they plenteously bringeth forth the fruits of good works;*
> *May of Thee be plenteously rewarded*

The Collect for the Sunday of Advent has been translated into a timely reminder to the housewives in the congregation to prepare the pudding, giving it time to mature before the Christmas feast. Father Charles Watson assured me that the Benedictine monks of Prinknash also gauge their preparations by the Collect *Excita, Quaerimus Domine*. 'Latin is such a beautiful language and that is probably why the church hangs on to it,' he says, 'Yes, we have a traditional Christmas dinner at midday, old-fashioned and made ourselves, everyone has already had a stir of the plum pudding on Stir-up Sunday.'

Christmas pudding was always referred to in times past as plum pudding, when all dried fruits were collectively called plums. In Cotswold dialect the fruits are known as 'feggy', often thought to mean figs, but as figs did not feature in the plum pudding it is more likely to mean the dried prunes (also referred to as plums, just to add to the confusion) which were an important addition to the porridge from which it all derived. Plum porridge was a Tudor conception of beef and veal boiled in spices and wine, usually hock or old sack, flavoured with citrus fruits and enriched, when cooked, with fried dried plums and dried grapes, sweetened with honey and thickened with crumbled coarse bread, to be served in a semi-liquid state. The rich pottage later became a filling for pies, but in Georgian times the meat element was replaced by suet (as in our now familiar mincemeat), the mixture thickened with a greater proportion of breadcrumbs and solidified with a little flour. The whole was then rolled into a large ball and boiled in a cloth. It was the Victorians who put the now recognisable Christmas

Feggy Dump.

pudding tidily into a basin and covered it with a cloth with the four corners tied in two knots opposite each other – which gives it such distinction, and a practical 'handle' for lifting it in and out of the steamer or boiler. Brown sugar, black treacle (originally just molasses), strong ale and long hours of steady boiling make this a truly traditional Cotswold Feggy Dump.

Dump is a boiled pudding – Feggy Dump is a richly fruited, spiced and booze-laden Christmas pudding. A Dunch Dump is a plain boiled pudding. Ag Pag Dump – such as the age old ditty says is the main diet of Nympsfield folk – means odds and ends (although many people insist it means 'heg-peg' – the ripe berries of the hawthorn bush, which I have always known as 'haws'). A pudding receipt dating back to the eighteenth century is probably more like the satirised Ag Pag Dump. This was made with barley, as 'boughten' ground flour was expensive. A cupful of barley was boiled until soft, then mixed with freshly picked, washed and chopped nettle tops, watercress, and the leaves of sorrel, mint, blackcurrant, wood garlic or an onion – whatever combinations were available. The mixture was bound together with an egg and about a tablespoonful of softened butter, moulded into a ball then placed in a well floured cloth, with the top tied tightly and boiled in the cast iron cooking pot suspended over the fire, along with a hunk of home-cured bacon and garden cabbage in its net.

> *Ov their furren tongues let travellers brag*
> *Wi' their vifteen names vor a puddin-bag*

These lines from an old ballad set the boiled-in-a-cloth pudding firmly on the English plate long before the Victorians 'invented' what they termed the Bolster Pudding. John Taylor, the Gloucester-born 'Water Poet', wrote in awe of Nicholas Wood, history's famous glutton, listing among the gourmand's diet *'the bag-puddings of Gloucestershire'*. This dates them to Elizabethan times. The English pudding was obviously something to be remarked upon, not just in nostalgic moments when serving 'the Queen Eliza', as Taylor did, but also by travellers 'with their furren tongue', for Masson, a mid-seventeenth-century French writer, recorded:

> The English are gluttons at noon and abstinent at night… Blessed be he that invented pudding, for it is a Manna that hits the palates of all sorts of people. Ah! What an excellent thing is an English pudding! To come in pudding time is as much as to say to come in the most lucky moment in the world.

No doubt foreigners had difficulty in keeping up with the different names 'vor a puddin-bag' if they came to the Cotswolds. As well as the Dumps, there is Hodge Podge, which is a black pudding, a savoury dish. Then there are Clangers, which are savoury, suet puddings incorporating scraps of bacon and chopped onion – rolled into a fat sausage shape and boiled in a cloth, like the famous Spotted Dick, but that is a sweet pudding, 'spotted' with sultanas and currants. Of course, the same pudding can be baked – but then it is a Duff and not a Dump!

J. Arthur Gibbs, in his classic portrayal of *A Cotswold Village,* at the end of the long Victorian era, relates the advice, given by Dr Johnson to his friends, always to have a good orchard attached to their house. 'For', said he, 'I once knew a clergyman of small income who brought up a family very reputably, which he chiefly fed on apple dumplings'. Apple dumplings, 'proper' ones, are made by encasing peeled and cored whole apples in puff pastry and baked. Wrapping the apple in suet crust and boiling it in a cloth is strictly not a dump – but a tantadlin. A suet crust 'lid' cooked directly on top of a beef in cider casserole is neither dump nor duff – but a skimmerlad!

Soul Cakes and Dumb Cakes and Holywake Bakes

> *A soul, a soul, a soul cake,*
> *Please, good Missus, a soul cake,*
> *An apple, pear, plum or cherry,*
> *Or anything to make us merry*

Soul cakes were the traditional 'reward' to the one time Soulers – very much like the mince pie became the customary offering to carol-singers who visited the 'big' houses to render a musical seasonal greeting. As with many cakes devised for festivals which had religious associations, the soul cake was spiced as a link with the spices brought to the Nativity. But the Old Soulers' verse was a kind of direct begging song seeking an edible payment for offering prayers for the departed on All Souls' Day, 2 November, and had its roots back to the Celtic tradition, following on from Halloween and All Saints Day. In the churchyard at Bisley there is a thirteenth-century Poor Souls' Light – thought to be the only one in England to be outside a church. Inside its carved stone spire top, candles were placed at Masses said for the collective poor of the parish. It stands on the site of an ancient well head, which became known locally as The Bonehouse. The story is that one dark night a priest was summoned to take the Blessed Sacrament to a parishioner, but never reached his destination. Later, his body was found at the foot of the well, and the parish was consequently excommunicated for a period. No burials were allowed in the churchyard, and the dead had to be carried to Bibury for interment. There is still a corner of Bibury churchyard called 'the Bisley Piece'. Another version of the story attributes the hapless victim to be a workman named Pierce who fell backwards into the well as the clock struck one!

Holywake Bakes have a completely unholy connotation. Holywake is a seventeenth-century word of the Cotswolds for bonfire, but not the autumnal burning of garden trumpery – it originated as the wakes held at the burning of heretics. As with public hangings, the spectacle attracted an audience and vendors had ready custom for their Holywake Bakes. Later, this gingerbread-type cake became the traditional fare for Bonfire Night.

Dumb Cakes got their rather curious name from the custom of being made on Christmas Eve in absolute silence by any spinster anxious to find some sign of whom her intended was to be. To speak to anyone during the making would be to break the magic spell she stirred into the mixture. She then scratched her initials on the top and left it to bake in the ashes of the fire when she retired to bed. The front door was left unlocked and at midnight a suitor would enter and prick his initials on top of the cake next to the hopeful cook's. On Christmas Day the suitor would return and watch for the lady's reaction. If she ate the cake – again

Skimmerlad casserole and Holywake Bake cake.

them in their slice of cake became King of the Bean and Queen of Marrowfat (Pea) for the evening, presiding in state over the programme of dancing and feasting. If the pea was found first by a man than he chose his queen; likewise, if a lady found the bean first then she elected her king.

Easter fare, like that of Christmas, incorporates some element of scriptural spices, but the way in which we celebrate Easter today is a curious admixture of pagan and Christian customs and country lore. The Cotswold housewife who baked her hot cross buns before attending Matins was not driven by piety, but by superstition – she did so as an insurance against her bread going mouldy throughout the year. One bun was hung in the ingle as a protection against the house burning down, and an extra large one was hidden away to insure against illness, and if some ailment eluded its magical charm, then the bun was crumbled up and mixed into a cup of water to be taken as a cure. Herbert Hedges, an old Headmaster of Fairford, had one such bun 'of inestimable age' that he had inherited as such a folk tale talisman – and he lived to be ninety-nine!

Several generations of schoolchildren at Stratton and Baunton, near Cirencester, have enjoyed a tradition of receiving a hot cross bun from The Plough at Stratton. This started out as a kind of insurance, too, when the landlord, Butcher Abgood, gave free buns on Good Friday just before the First World War to the local children as a bribe to stop them knocking his haycocks down in the paddock. The custom was only halted temporarily when rationing imposed its own strictures. The spiced bun was always the subject of superstition. Medieval bakers marked their bread with a cross to ward off the evil eye and to encourage it to rise. The custom was declared 'popish' at the Reformation, and only the buns made on Good Friday were allowed to be crossed – symbolic of the Crucifixion.

The Jewish sacrificial lamb for their Passover feast, called the Paschal Lamb, became part of the Christian feast fare, and the pagans honoured *Eostre,* the Saxon goddess of Spring, by including eggs in their celebratory feasting as symbols of re-birth after the long, dreary and dead months of winter. Traditional Easter Day dinner in the Cotswolds has been roast lamb and baked egg custard and tansy pudding for centuries. Cakes were also flavoured with the rather bitter juice of tansy and awarded as prizes at Easter revels and sports.

A custom which seemed to belong more to the north than the south of the region was that of farmers burying a piece of simnel cake in the corner of their land, then pouring cider over it to ensure a good crop in the coming season. The simnel cake, with its characteristic almond paste covering decorated with eleven balls to signify the disciples (Judas, the traitor, is pointedly omitted), has been adopted as a traditional Easter cake.

It truly belongs earlier to Mothering Sunday. Herrick set the custom in its original context:

I'll to thee a simnel bring
'Gainst thou go a-mothering
So that when she blesses thee
Half that blessing you'll give me.

Mothering Sunday centred round the mother church of the parish, when congregations from smaller churches visited to pay their respects in medieval times. By the Elizabethan period 'Mother' was associated with parentage and probably got further confused with Lady Day on 25 March, which celebrated the Mother of God. It later became the day when servant girls and bound apprentices were allowed home to visit their mothers; girls in domestic service took a simnel cake, which they had baked as proof of their acquired culinary skills. Mothers reciprocated by preparing for their children a special dish of frumenty – a kind of citrus-flavoured junket made from soaked cracked wheat. In the Stroud Valleys, where it was called Fermitty, the dish was taken round to share with friends as well as family.

Whit Wakes and Wap Whipot

May Day ranked high in the pre-Christian festivals, heralding in the Spring with the maypole as an enduring centrepiece of the revelling and dancing celebrations. May walking and 'knocking up the trees from their winter slumber' lingered well into living memory on the hills and wolds. As dawn breaks over Oxford, the choristers of Magdalen College greet the day from the top of the tower with the Latin hymn, *Te Deum Patrem colimus*, which is part of the College Grace and dates back to the seventeenth century, although the custom itself is thought to go back to at least the time of Henry VIII.

May was always a merry month with its Wakes, or Patronal Feasts, known as Revels, and Whitsuntide crowds the Cotswold calendar with a whole range of customs. Whit Ales were originally means of fund-raising for the church and often referred to as Church Ales, providing alms for the poor and helping with maintenance costs of the church itself before rates were introduced. To the parishioners they were eagerly awaited occasions for social gatherings, sports, singing, dancing and general jolly junketings.

The famous Cotswold 'Olympick' Games, or Dover's Games as they were often called after their founder Robert Dover, were first instituted

in Whit week in 1612 and extended the Chipping Campden Whitsun
Ale into revels of sporting games such as hare-coursing, shin-kicking,
jousting and breaking heads with cudgels just for the fun of it all; for
the weaker in strength and spirit there were dancing and card games.
Dover's Games and Scuttlebrook Wake are legendary in their range and
popularity.

Eastward across the hills the Cooper's Hill Wake keeps up tradition
with the ancient custom of cheese-rolling, one of the few such cere-
monies to survive in the kingdom. Its origins are shrouded in hoary
half-beliefs and superstition. So, for example, one can choose between a
pagan ritual of trying to arrest the sun in an annual saturnalia, symbol-
ised by folk risking life and limb hurtling down a one-in-one gradient
of Cooper's Hill while trying to catch the seven-pound cheese (Double
Gloucester, of course) before it reaches the bottom, or a hairy way of
establishing ancient grazing rights on the common land. A handbill
sent to the Town Crier of Gloucester to 'cry' the annual sports of
Whitsuntide 1836 gives a fascinating glimpse of the country fun of
the day:

Cooper's Hill Weke to commence on Wits Monday

Persisly at 3 o'clock.

2 cheese to be ron for

1 Plain cake to be green for

1 do. Do. To be jumpt in the bag for

Horings to be Dipt in the toob for

Set of ribbons to be dansed for

Shimey to be ron for

Belt to be rosled for

A bladder of snuff to be

Chatred for by hold wimming

Dipping in the tub for oranges, dancing for ribbons, wrestling for a
belt, running for a chemise, the grinning (through a horse's collar) and
the 'chattering by old women' for a bladder of snuff have been replaced
by a tug-of-war and scrambling for sweets by the maypole in more recent
times.

Cheese-rolling at Randwick has more ecclesiastical connections with
a church service on the first Sunday in May – it used to be a May Day
celebration – where three Double Gloucester cheeses are rolled round
the church three times, in an anti-clockwise direction, by those present
forming a ring. The cheese, from the rolling, is cut up and distributed at
the Wap. Runnick Wap, as it is locally known, survives today as a country

Maypole dancers heralded in the spring festivals – here they are transported as a tableau before performing at Fairford Carnival, in around 1925.

fair, the highlight of which is the ancient mayor election ceremony, with High Sheriff, Swordbearer, Mopman and a Wap Queen with her attendants. The cheeses are carried on a flower-decked litter during a colourful and fun-filled day held now on the second Saturday in May. Samuel Rudder wrote of the Wap in the late eighteenth century as 'an ancient custom'. It survived the puritanical suppression of lively Revels and Wakes with their licence for intemperance.

Rudder's description of Childwickham's Wake, which dated 'from time immemorial' is interesting insofar as it gives a look at the fare of his day:

> The Lord of the Manor gives a certain quantity of malt to brew ale to be given away at Whitsuntide and a certain quantity of flour to make cakes; everyone who keeps a cow sends curds, others plums, sugar and flour; and the payers to church and poor contribute 6d each towards furnishing out an entertainment, to which every poor person of the parish who comes, has, with a quart of ale a cake, a piece of cheese, and a cheesecake.

Cheesecakes for Whitsun Ales were mentioned as early as 1634, when a miller at Churchdown 'made large preparation (for 'a solemn' Whitsun Ale) even of threescore dozen cheesecakes'. Possibly the earliest mention of cheesecake is one of 1265 when soft curds were listed for tarts. Curd cheesecakes of ewe's milk were a staple diet for Cotswold shepherds at shearing time.

Notwithstanding the fact that it is the local cheese that is the focus of the Randwick Wap, it is not cheesecake that is the customary fare but Whipot, or White Pot, Pout or Put, with as many variations on its theme as its spelling – from a porridgy-type of baked custard, or a stick-to-your-ribs bread pudding, to a baked sop. Even in John Smyth's chronicles in the *Berkeley Manuscripts* written in the seventeenth century, there is room for individual interpretation:

> Hee is very good at white pott. By white pot, wee westerners doe meane a great custard or puddinge baked in a bagg, platter, kettle or pan; notinge heerby, a good trencher man, or great eater.

Wap Whipot, established over the last three decades by Pat Ballinger, was based on her research into the Wap history. After trying to decipher what made the Randwick White Pot special, she guessed that the 'secret ingredient' was home-made wine and incorporated it in her mother's celebrated bread pudding recipe, making it in the old-fashioned deep earthenware crock in the time-honoured way to great success.

8

MAKING MUSIC

SONG, DANCE & MUMMING

'Please to let the Mummers in'. These words were as much a part of Christmas as the holly and ivy that decked the halls, where the ancient folk play took place in almost every village in the Cotswolds until the First World War. Now, barely a handful of bands of mummers weave their old-time magic with the curious tongue-twisting dialogue, fanciful disguise and general buffoonery interplay leading up to a knockabout fight between the goodie and the baddie. The miraculous recovery of the slain villain of the piece through the quackery of the doctor is the nucleus of the play, symbolising the resurrection of the dying year to live anew in the coming new year. Although treated as the most farcical character, with his Renaissance mountebank-style stock boasting of his powers, his role is related to that of the primitive medicine man and therefore is a pivotal part of the play. Play, in fact, is rather a grandiose term for what is really a folk fertility ritual with pagan roots. It was the Christians who introduced the moral fight of good against evil. Characters have often changed over the centuries to personify contemporary adversaries: the earliest pair being St George and the Dragon, later replaced by a Turkish Knight or 'Belzebub', the Devil, who appeared some time after the medieval Miracle Plays. The tales of folk heroes such as Robin Hood oppose all kinds of storybook 'bad' characters, or any political figure worthy of lampooning with impunity, regardless of logical, chronological or historical association.

Disguise is more important than theatrical-type costume, hence many players appear with blackened faces – now resorting to greasepaint as an easier alternative to the once traditional burnt cork. Anonymity of the player is all important – 'Old Whose-It-from-Down-the-Road' he may be all the year, but as a mummer he is a mysterious, comical figure weaving a magic in a seasonal ritual of long ago. Costume as such usually consisted of making do with whatever dress came to hand, with many favouring the white trousers and shirts of the Morris dancers; others kept to smocks. Exception is made for the Doctor, by custom, distinguished as quasi-professional – although memories of South Cerney's 'Quack', played by 'Dr' Bateman, revealed that he sported rather incongruous white hunting breeches with his frock coat and top hat. Performed regularly until 1913, other players included G. Taylor, T. and F. Price, L. Legg, A. Dunn and G. Maidment. It appears that there was a close tie with, or even evolvement from, morris dancing, as they had a Fool and danced 'Bacca Pipe's Jig' over swords, ending with 'Maid o' the Mill'. Their traditional song was 'Brandon on the Moor', but 'the words were lost by the present generation by 1913'.

Distinctive disguise singles out the famous 'Paper Boys' of the Marshfield Mummers, whose coats and hats are completely covered in coloured strips of paper. Kempsford players make a token gesture to their predecessors by wearing waistcoats decorated with strips of coloured material, representing the river reeds once worn in this Upper Thames village.

Mumming died out because it is a purely oral tradition. The plays were acted out by local people and passed down the generations simply by learning the lines by heart in the best tradition of folklore, tales and song and many were lost with the men who died in the First World War. They were never designed as stage plays, although a manuscript journal of a company 'led by one Mr Jones' makes mention of performing 'for trifling profits' at Faringdon and Lechlade; among the troupe's repertoire of abridged versions of a couple of Shakespearian plays was 'an enter-tainment featuring St George and a Mock Doctor'. It is from the scraps of dialogue and long memories that revivals have been reconstructed. Marshfield was the only village in Gloucestershire where 'Mummerie', as it used to be called, was regularly performed as a revival from 1931 until 1969 when Waterley Bottom Mummers were formed. It was by chance that Marshfield's vicar of that time, the Reverend C. Alford, overheard his gardener reciting some lines of doggerel and mentioned it

Waterley Bottom Mummers performing outside Dursley church in the early seventies.

to his sister, Violet Alford, an eminent folklorist, who identified them as fragments of a mummer's play. Her scholarly knowledge and collecting of memories from the older residents, enabled her to reconstruct the famous play with three of the company taking part who had been mummers in Victoria's day.

Waterley Bottom, lying between Wotton-under-Edge and Dursley, was chosen as the appropriate name for the company drawn from both towns when it was formed in 1969. Their performance ends with the Gloucestershire Wassail Song, which Richard Chidlaw told me was sung to him by an old lady from Tresham. The wassail bowl is the original one from Hillesley, and mulled cider made to a secret recipe is drunk from its four lips. The bowl had been rescued from its role as a container for growing geraniums, and the concept of a revival of the Dursley Mummers' Play was credited to Brian Hayward, English Master at Wotton, following an interest in an essay on the tradition in Gloucestershire, and, again, the interest of a local vicar who wrote down the words around 1883.

All of us who are keen folklorists have been collecting the words of the old mummers plays to ensure they are not lost entirely and so they appear in script form which would have been quite alien to the old bands who simply 'says it as a–allus bin sed'.

Sherborne Mummers' Play
(Recalled by Jack Saunders in 1980)

Knock on the door. Father Christmas is the leader and speaks first
for them all.

Father Christmas
Please to let the Mummers act.
In comes I, old Hindbefore. I come forrard to open the door
In comes I, Old Father Christmas, welcome here or welcome not
I hope old Father Christmas will never be forgot.
I brought a besom to sweep your house
I brought a besom to kick up a dust
I pray Good Master and Good Missus, I hope you're both within
I comes this Merry Christmas time to show you kith and kin
And if you take it as offence, pray tell it unto me
And I will be quickly gone or hence
A room, a room for my brave gallant men, I come this Merry Christmas time to
*   show you activity*
Activity of youth, activity of age
I'll show you all the prettiest actions you ever saw
Acted upon a common stage.

David Brand
I'm a tanner, a tanner from Hampshire, my name is David Brand
There's not a man in Gloucestershire that's made Old David stand
As I walked up and down Farmington Grove, there I met a red deer
I waved my staff and he flew away
My staff in length is three foot five and a half
And he'll knock down a calf, I'll warrant he'll knock down you
So let all your voices ring
Please to let in the Prooshun King.

Prussian King
I am the Royal Prooshun King, many a red battle have I been in
Fighting for George our King
If this is not true I am mistaken or what makes me carry this red waven
Be it French, Spaniard or Turk I know there's no man here can do me hurt
Hack him and hew him as small as a fly, I'd send him to Satan to make a mince
*   pie*
Mince pies hot, mince pies cold, I'd send him to Satan afore he was nine days old
So let all your voices ring – I am the Royal Prooshun King.

Father Christmas
If this is not true, as I have been told, come in the valiant soldier bold.

Soldier
I am the gallant soldier bold – Bold Slasher is my name
My sword and buckle by my side, I long to win this game
French Officer, French Officer am I
Long time I've driven these fields so fly
So now I think I've a right to try, to see which on the ground shall lie
So here's the man that bade me stand
Said he'd knock me down with his right and gracious hand
Said he'd hack me and hew me, as small as flies
Said he'd send me to Satan to make mince pies
Mince pies hot, mince pies cold, he said he'd send me to Satan
Before I was nine days old.

They start fighting; after a bit, Old Woman comes in unbidden and gestures with her broomstick.

Father Christmas
Hello Old Ooman, what brings you here?

Old Woman
Me legs.

Father Christmas
Ought to be home, mending thee rags.

Old Woman
Twixt thee and the doctor, I've only had one drink of gin this week
Physica, physica broomstick
Cut away boys, cut away.

The Prussian King is down. Old Woman kneels beside him holding his head. The Doctor is still offstage; when he first speaks it is to Jack Finney.

Father Christmas
Doctor, Doctor, come and see. King George is wounded through the knee
Doctor, Doctor, do thy part King George is wounded through the heart.'

A German professor at Oxford is said to have asked an old Mummer during the thirties if women ever took part. 'No, sir,' the man replied, 'It aint for the likes of a 'ooman, Mumming be more like parson's work.'

Breaking with that tradition, both Diana Cox and I not only resurrected and wrote a Mummers' Play, but also acted in them for our respective communities. Diana had been shown a copy of the Kempsford version which had been recorded in 1868, taken from John Couling, whose family could be traced back through the village records for centuries. She formed a new group and they have performed her slightly shortened version intermittently since 1983, taking over for Kempsford where I left off for Fairford, having written and performed our version a decade before; again, cobbling together fragments of the curious dialogue and interplay, common and unique to all.

Of course, it is all illegal! Mummery comes under the terms of masques, which along with 'revelling, epicurisme, dancing, drinking, stage plaies and carnale pomp and jollity' were banned by the Puritans and the law was never taken off the Statute Book. But the law also states that a Christmas dinner must not exceed three courses, men cannot be shaved or have a hair-cut on Christmas Day, when sport is curtailed to practising archery – although one can 'vault' or 'leap' with impunity! An Act of 1551 states that folk should walk to church; any carriage found near the church can be confiscated, and not attending at least one service on Christmas Day carries a fine of one shilling. None of the above laws has ever been repealed – meanwhile we carry on mumming and making merry!

The fight between good and bad characters – the core of all Mumming plays.

A Merry Come Up of Morris

'A merry come up' is an old Cotswold expression of the 'merrimen' (morris men), who provided the musical entertainment throughout the region, with a tradition that stretches back many centuries. The Cotswold type was very distinctive: a set of six dancers with bells, according to Dr Russell Wortley, whose researches into the various bands of morris extended into tracing the families of recorded Morris men. One name that runs through the branches of the family trees of traditional 'merrimen' is that of Hathaway. William Hathaway 'of Cheltenham' added to Cecil Sharp's famed collection in 1908 by saying that: 'Morris was danced at Bledington, Kingham, Lower Guiting (accompanied by tabor and pipe), Sherborne ("a desperate Morris place") and Leafield ("A great Morris place near Shipton under Wychwood"). James Bennet, a tall man hailing from Stow went to Bidford some thirty years earlier and started them on Morris dancing'. According to *Birmingham Weekly Post,* 'Notes and Queries', 'dancing Cotswold Morris was last recorded at Stow-on-the-Wold in 1885/86'.

Mrs Hathaway of Lower Swell, sister-in-law of the fiddler (William, previously quoted, who returned to Lower Swell in his later years) again verified that the Cotswold Morris team comprised 'six men, a fool, music and a man with a box', and described the customary white shirts as having 'a straight pleat down centre with little frills on each side; four or five tucks on each side, very narrow, as narrow as could be done. The frill being about an inch broad – but not all of them have them, but the best ones do.' Her husband 'used to go and do Merrimen Fool, but was sometimes called Martha or Squire instead. He always blacked his face and carried a stick – on one end a bladder, on the other a calf's tail. They had a good merry up'. This must have been William's brother, who was known by his nickname Nobby, whose escapades as Morris Fool were remembered well into the thirties. Henry Hathaway, another brother, danced with the Longborough side under Harry Taylor – the last landlord of the (now demolished) pub behind the old Post Office in Lower Swell.

The most authenticated Cotswold-type tradition of morris to survive the longest belongs to Latton, just north of the Thames as it skirts the valley plains to return to the Cotswolds again at Lechlade. The river is generally accepted as marking the southern boundary of the Cotswold traditional folk dance territory. An area within a thirty-mile radius of Stow-on-the-Wold was for centuries the ancient home of morris dancing in the south of England, and it was from here that the history of the teams has been garnered.

Merriman was the name by which the Fool of the Naunton Morris men was known. They also wore pleated shirts, but without frills, hard silk hats with ribbon streamers, silk neckerchiefs, white cord breeches and bells on their shins. Charles Hughes was recorded as selling William Hathaway of Cheltenham his first fiddle in exchange for a pair of boots worth 3s 6d:

> It was a good fiddle. My pipe was made by Danley of Andoversford, from whom Carter bought it. It was not a new one then and always bound at bottom. Made of plum wood. The tabor was made by Carter himself. He got the parchment from an old drum and had the iron rings cast by an iron man at Bourton. David Dankey was the pipe man.

The Travelling Morrice made their first tour in 1924, taking dances back to their roots and searching out as many surviving members of the old teams as they could find to record their music and dances; a valuable addition to the collections made by Cecil Sharp. Generally, the repertoire is incredibly wide-ranging; locally the versions are fascinatingly unique, and, as in all good folklore traditions, are developed by the individuals who performed them. The Bledington Morris in particular took Cecil Sharp's fancy as being 'evidently a very rustic morris set and one of the highest of interest'. Some two decades after Sharp had published his findings, the Travelling Morrice performed the Bledington dances, as published, in their pioneering tour in front of a few of the original dancers. But there were three points on which the local men independently declared the performances differed from their own practice: 'first, the Bledington dancers did not bend forward in the fore-capers; secondly, they kicked forward but not back in the uprights; and, thirdly, there was no shuffle back in the half-gip'.

Dr Russell Wortley, a member of the Travelling Morrice, assumed that for the purpose of publication, Sharp had decided to assimilate the 'split-jump uprights' of the Sherborne Morris into the Bledington version. For those who so much enjoy watching these ancient dances, which might well be reckoned as a small team of ribbon-hatted and bell-legged chaps having a jolly knees-up to some catchy country tunes, interspersed by a bladder-waving Fool clowning around amid a lot of hanky waving, a cursory glance at Dr Wortley's description of the stages in the recover of the Bledington dance tradition sounds as complicated as any ballet choreography. 'No use kicking back in the upright capers', George Hathaway explained to me, using his fingers to illustrate what he meant, that the feet must be crossed three times in preparation for the jump. Experiment shows that on the third cross-hop a firm toe-tap will substantially assist

Cotswold Morris has a long tradition in our folklore.

the spring and forward thrust of the free leg prior to landing on it on the final beat. He was particularly familiar with the leap-frog dance which was known as the 'Glorisher', and insisted that all the jumps should be at the top of the set. They bent down with their back towards the man about to jump – not broadside on. George Hathaway and Lewis Hall spoke of 'hook-leg and hey', never 'hey and hook-leg', and it was thus that the 'hook-leg into the hey' in half-hey dances was established. I was further told to swing my leg as near the ground as possible in the hook-leg. It is the initial swing of the free foot (as though on the end of a piece of string) which gives most of the rotary impulse which turns the dancer round during a galley or hook-leg. Hook-legs do not come into the jigs, George told me, 'you must wriggle your feet back'. In 'hook-legging', partners always work together – 'more noble', was his way of describing the effect. This rule should apply even to the salute in 'Trunkles'.

'Trunkles', 'William and Nancy', 'The Gallant Hussar' and 'Leap-Frog' were just four parts of the dance repertoire, with jigs fascinatingly named 'Princess Royal', 'Ladies Pleasure' and 'Lumps of Plum Pudding' performed by the Bledington Morris. Charles Benfield, a fiddler of the 'old' side, spoke of the tradition lapsing for some two decades before Sharp started his collection, but helped to train a 'young' side of which George Hathaway and Lewis Hall were members until 'the young side finally gave up owing to the opposition of stall-holders at village fairs, who drowned their music with rattles, their last appearance being at

Fifield Club'. George lent his treasured heart-shaped Bledington collecting tin to the Travelling Morrice during the whole of their tour in 1946. Among the other places from which dances and songs were collected by this branch of the Cambridge Morris Men, who toured the area contributing so much to the history of the tradition, were Longborough, Chipping Campden, Stow-on-the-Wold, Chadlington, Headington Quarry and Bampton.

Bampton-in-the-Bush Morris Men, to give them the original town name, reckon 'as far as is known', to have some six hundred years of unbroken tradition, according to Ray Borrett, their present-day Fool. One of barely a handful of the real Cotswold teams to survive with such a pedigree, Bampton Morris perform only the dances from their own historic tradition, whereas many teams do a multiplicity of dances and 'go by the book'. Their repertoire of some twenty dances follow the same movements, but, as Ray explained, 'the accents are different and so the dance is evolving all the time, this is what makes it a living tradition rather than a dead one'. The Fool has a dance of his own to the melodeon and also to the fiddle. Bampton's custom is to dance on the streets on only one day of the year – on old Whit Monday. There are similarities to a Horn Dance, and an old bell pad in Oxford Museum shows its 'bells' were made from cowrie shells. Chastising with a bladder on the end of a stick is universal and many authorities root the morris back to Moorish origins, while others attribute its origins to a pagan celebration of Ceres, the goddess of grain. The ritual is the strongest tradition and the nucleus of any dance; with the symbolic circling at the end of the dance to exclude the Devil. Bampton dance in traditional smocks, with the front and back alike from the time when they were the practical dress of the country worker – the cleanest side being turned to the front for Sunday church-going. It is said that old Shepherd Hayward of Bampton was buried in his smock. No doubt he also had a lock of sheep's wool pinned on his chest as a token of his calling, so that when he arrived at the pearly gates his absence from regular church services was excused on account of his duty to his flock. The late Frank Williams, a stalwart member of the Cotswold Sheep Society and a notable breeder of the noble and indigenous breed, recently followed the age-old custom of being buried with a lock of wool from his beloved Cotswold sheep. Traditional style calico smocks, windproof and practical for their original purpose as a working overgarment, are, as Ray says, very hot for dancing in, and far from being 'posey prancing' as some may term morris dancing, it is a very strenuous activity – anyone trying just three minutes on spongy grass at a village fair will appreciate that and, despite its antiquity, this curious and quaint custom still attracts a following of young people.

Bampton Morris has a pedigree dating back some six centuries.

Going through the steps at Kempsford School.

Songs as Sung, Collected and Concocted

Gwain to Cizzeter Mop

We aal be gwain to Cizzeter Mop
On Munday marn so jolly,
Along wi' Bill an' Carter Joe
An' Lizer Jane and Molly.

We aal turn'd out in clane white smocks
An' billycocks so grand,
An' Joe he twisted whip cord
Aal roun' him vor a band.

Twur girt big blue an' yeller vlowers
Was in our Lizer's hat;
Bill show'd out in his karderoys,
Red 'ankerchif an' that.

The volks did stir as we wur gwain,
An' many 'ollered out –
"Go an' get hir'd at Cizzeter,
Ya lumbrin' country lout".

We walk'd aal droo the noisy Mop
Along wi' Bill and Molly,
An' seed the wenches stan' for hire
In aal thur fol-de-rolly

An' thur wur Serney men an' bwoys,
Wi' girls from Ashun Kaynes;
An' Barnsley volks cum ridin' in
A waggin wi'out reins.

Cheap Jack, he wur a sellin' nives,
An' wink's his eye at I,
He draad the nife rite up an' down
An' ask'd, "who wants to die?"

Uh sed the nife ud cut it fat
An' purpose made for I;
A country bumpkin, Chawbacon,
The bwoys thay aal did cry.

The painted 'osses twirlin' roun'
Close by the irun pump,
Was rode by Joe an' Lizer Ann –
They fell off, sich a vlump.

A soljur wi' his bagginit
An' ribbons aal so vine,
Clapt I upon the back, an' sed,
"Bee Jarge, an' thee mus' jine".

"I byent gwain to 'list," sez I,
"For Queen, nor King, today
I'z gwain whoam wi' Varmer Turk
To drive 'is team vor pay".

While the sarjen' was a taulkin' loud
'Bout regiment an' the penshun,
Punch an' Judy – thay march'd by
An' 'tracted aal th' 'tenshun.

An' when Jack Ketch brung up the gallows
To 'ang the rascal Punch,
Punch pulls the string an' ketches 'im
An' makes un veel zo dunch.

Wen Punch an' Judy shut up shop
We wen' down to the shows;
An' wa-wi' noisy drums an' 'orns
Thay kik'd up nashun rows.

The pictures aal 'ung out in vront,
An' beasts did roar zo loud;
Lor, wat a janglin' zound thur wur,
An' wat a mortal kroud.

The man up top, he 'ollered out
"Ye need not veel alarm,
Cum zee the roorin' lions jump
Droo hoops an' then perfurm".
The peep-shows an' the waxen dolls,
The vat bwoy an' the peg;

We aal went in, a penny each,
The vat bwoy show'd his leg.

Thay aal zung out, "Walk up, walk up"
Wen volks were cumin out;
An' at the sparrin' tent, "Cum in –
An' 'ave a fitin' bout".

An' further down twur singing zongs
'Bout wiskee, gin, an' rum;
Thay want'd I to buy a ditty
About the "Harvest Whoam".

We went into the Dree Kauks Inn
An' had a pint o' ale,
An' call'd to zee the old Black 'Oss,
The King's Arms an' the Bell.

Twur late wen we got on the road
Wi' Lizer, Jane and Joe,
An' found our way to village whoam
Vrom Cizzeter Mop to gwoa.

This wonderful word picture of a day at Cirencester Mop as a forum for hiring farm hands and maid servants, among the mêlée of a country town fair and recruiting ground for the militia, recorded in local dialect is one of the best forms of the ballad tradition. Catching contemporary happenings in a sing-song verse, sung to any folk tune that fitted the stanza, gives life to a cherished oral tradition, and so it was with the Wyck Rissington version of the old song 'Gossip Joan', sung to the tune which is to be found in several ballad-operas which H.H. Albino collected from Thomas Lanchbury in 1928 as the song *Good morning, Gossip Jones*. Thomas Lanchbury was then about sixty years old and worked as a cowman; his reference to his cow calving under the parlour window – 'And we shall have some cherry curds for breakfast in the morning, Gossip Jones' – had the ring of authenticity as the 'cherry curds' (beestings), the first rich and creamy milk after calving, was always the cowman's perks and made the most delicious kind of baked custard. Thomas Lanchbury also 'belonged to the tower', as local church bell-ringers were termed. His memory of the home-made fiddle that accompanied the local Morris dancing was that of two tins fixed at either end of a strip of wood with a whipcord stretched across from one tin to the

'Jenny sits a-weeping', one of the Little Rissington singing games revived by Canon Cheales, performed at the church patronal festival in the seventies.

other. A bow was used, but 'there wasn't much of a tune about it, it just kept the dancers going'.

Among the songs of the Cotswolds collected by Cecil Sharp were:

'New Garden Fields' from Henry Thomas of Chipping Sodbury, 1907.

'The Hermit' from William Sparrow of Kemble, 1913.

'T for Thomas' from Kathleen Williams, a gypsy of Wigpool Common, 1921.

'Beautiful Nancy' from Mrs P. Wiggett of Ford, 1909.

'The Seven Joys of Mary' from Joseph Evans of Old Sodbury, 1907.

'Three Pretty Maidens' from William Hedges of Chipping Campden, 1909.

'The Virgin Unspotted', and 'The Orange and Blue' from Mrs E. Smitherd of Tewkesbury, 1908.

'The Leather Bottle', and 'A Sweet Country Life' from William Henry Watts of Tewkesbury, 1908.

'Botany Bay' from Richard Toms of Cirencester Workhouse, 1911.

Continuity of collecting folk songs and music is paramount to their preservation, and even more valuable to our heritage of social history and Cotswold

culture is the performing of them – such as is practised by Richard Chidlaw
of the Waterley Bottom Mummers. Among his collection are vignettes of
working life, such as 'The Shepherd's Song', Tresham version sung by William
Chappell, and 'Granny Francom's father'. Gran's recollections of it was, 'An'
ah-did kip on repeatin' on it – drove I mad'! 'The Crow-Clapping Song',
sung by N.H.K. Pilsworth of Woodfield in 1971 was taught to him by his
father, Bill Pilsworth, who sang it as a boy in the fields of Petty France and
Badminton on his first job as a bird-scarer:

> *Shee-auver birds, shee-auver birds,*
> *Out of the cornfields and clover,*
> *Powder and shot shall be your lot,*
> *Shee-auver birds.*

Some songs are precious by being a composition concocted in recognition of a local event or personal contribution to a community, like 'The
Dursley Mummers', sung by B.J. Hayward at Wickwar in 1970, taking a
humorous look at their origins and the role played by Richard Chidlaw
(referred to as R.P.C. in the first verse).

Chorus:
Shut your windows, bar your doors, put your cider out of sight,
Hide away your daughter and turn out all the light,
And when the door goes ★ ★ ★, don't let in kith nor kin,
Vor the Dursley Mummers are out tonight, and they're wanting to come in.

We've had a strange eventful time, in this locality,
Since the band of Dursley Mummers was enrolled by R.P.C.
Things have been found missing, objects lost from sight,
Riots and disturbances, apparitions out of night.

It started down at Frampton, on a farm not far from here,
A farmer had a famous bull, its prowess all too clear,
But when the TV cameras and the Press men came to see
They only found the torso – for the head, ask R.P.C.

They found a stone at Cadbury, when digging Arthur's hill,
Excalibur was stuck in it, what an archaeological thrill!
They couldn't pull the sword out, so they left it in the dirt,
Andrew nicked it straight away, to use for Bonapert.
Richard wanted Mummers' garb, and a wassail bowl to way,
So he and his merry men went to Blaise Museum one day.

The curator eyed them carefully, and checked on all the locks,
But he lost a wooden chamber pot, and half a dozen smocks.

Last Christmastime, like the Three Wise Men, they made for the Star
Immediately they marched in and wassailed round the bar.
And when the Broad was carried in at Wotton-under-Edge,
The customers ran out screaming, and Bill Shellard signed The Pledge.

An instance illustrating how an oral tradition has wrought its own changes through the generations is in the corruption of the name 'Wassail', when Richard recorded the words of the Tresham Wassail in 1969. Mrs Alice Frankcom and Mrs Sally Dickenson joined in the singing of the words given by Granny Frankcom but, as she said, 'You got to fit your own tune to'n', then Gran started it off:

We'll sail, we'll sail all over the town
Our toast it is white, and the ale it is brown,
Our bowl it is made of the malpalin tree,
And a walsailin' bowl we'll drink unto thee

Gran consistently sang 'walsail' for 'wassail' and at one stage chided her daughter and daughter-in-law: 'What be singin' it s'posh for?' This is reminiscent of another old Cotswold character, the likes of which we shall never see again, 'Our Ame' – Miss Amy Cook of Wotton-under-Edge, a road sweeper of note whose deep dialectical phrases brought a smile to those who knew her and a dazed look of incomprehension to those who 'dussn't spake like us do'. 'Yes,' Amy is caught on a recording as saying, 'I can say Good morning, and how are you; but I can also say Marnin' an' how bist thee'. It is by recording the comments, particularly Granny Frankcom's, that give Richard Chidlaw's collection, which he entitled *A Gloucestershire Entertainer, produced by R P C 1975 for the Wicked Old Toads*, such charm, and one can sense the old lady's tone of voice in some of them. 'Late Home Came I', sung by Alice, her daughter-in-law, was obviously one that Gran did not totally approve of, 'If you don't want that you can burn it,' she advised.

Like many folk songs, there is the occasional earthy verse to keep the men guffawing over their ale pots, and the ladies blushing and fussing into their hankies. There was obviously no censorious Granny to tut-tut as Uncle Joe Wytchard of North Nibley contributed his version of 'Buttercup Joe'.

Now I be a rustic sort of chap, me mother lives o'er Fareham,
Where all the girls wear calico drawers, an' I knows how to tear'm
Some they calls I Bacon Fat, and other Turnip Head,
But I prove to you I be no fool, because I'm country bred.

Chorus:
Now I can guide a plough, milk a cow, and I can reap and sow,
Fresh as the daisies in the field, and they calls I Buttercup Joe

The tale goes on to tell of rough and tumbles in the hay and his young woman, Mary, who works 'in Farmer Jones's dairy'.

Cecil King of Kempsford, a notable folk-singer and mummer of his time, wrote down the words for me of the version sung in the south-eastern corner of the Cotswolds:

Buttercup Joe

I'm a true bred country chap, my father comes from Fareham
My mother has some more like I, and knows well how to rare um.
Some people calls I Bacon Fat, others Turnip Fed,
I'll prove to you I aint as flat, though I be country bred.

Chorus:
I can drive a plough, milk a cow, I can reap and mow
I am fresh as the daisies that grow in the field, and they calls I Buttercup Joe.

Have you seen my young woman, they calls her our Mary
She works as busy as a bumble bee down in Johnson's dairy
And don't she bake those dumplings nice
By Jove I means to try um
And ask her how she'd like to wed a country chap as I am.

Some folks they like hay making, others they like mowing
But of all the jobs I like best is a bit of turnip hoeing,
And shan't I be glad when I get wed to my old Mary Ann
I work for her and do my best, to please her all I can.

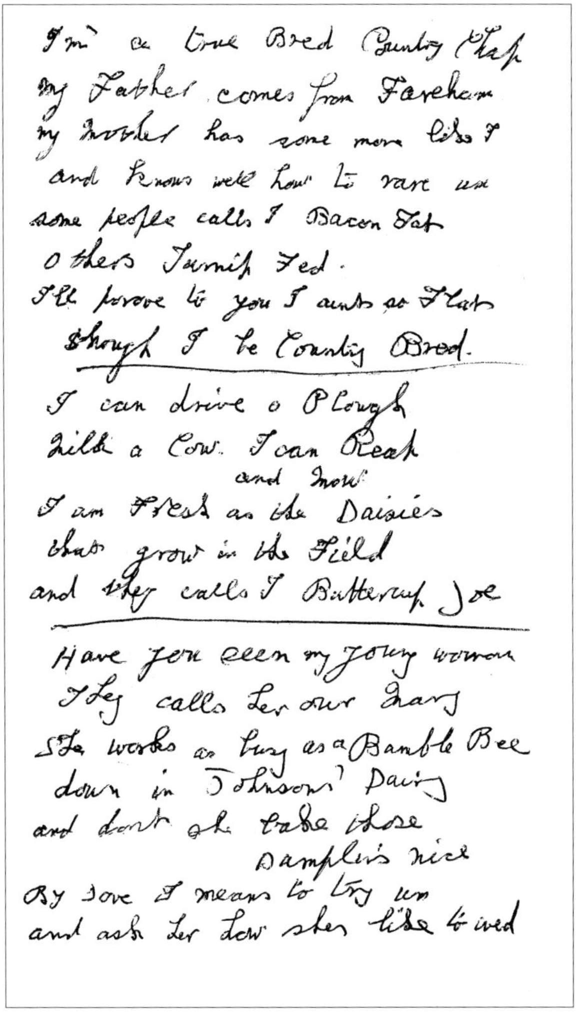

I'm a true Bred Country Chap
my Father comes from Fareham
my mother has some more like I
and knows well how to rare um
some people calls I Bacon Fat
others Turnip Fed.
I'll prove to you I aint so Flat
though I be Country Bred.

I can drive o Plough
Milk a Cow. I can Reap
and mow
I am Fresh as the Daisies
that grow in the Field
and they calls I Buttercup Joe

Have you seen my Young woman
They calls her our Mary
She works as busy as a Bumble Bee
down in Johnson' Dairy
and dont she make those
Dumplins nice
By Jove I means to try um
and ask her how she like to wed

'And they calls I Buttercup Joe' – from Cecil King's notebook.

Making Music Wherever They Go

So from villages three and four miles away come bands of children to sing the old, old songs. The brass band, including old grey-haired men who fifty years ago with strings and woodwind led the psalmody at Chedworth church, come too, and play inside the hall.

So wrote J. Arthur Gibbs a century ago, of Christmas at Ablington Manor in the Coln Valley. Making music wherever they went were the village musicians of yesteryear, often literally playing or singing for their supper. They were in demand to accompany country dancing, whether

Village bands were in great demand to head all the social gatherings – as here in Fairford, c. 1910.

Chedworth Band, photographed in 1879, at what was probably a Friendly Society meeting, and would have been the village band immortalised by J. Arthur Gibbs as playing at Ablington Manor.

Still very much a part of the Cotswold tradition, the present Chedworth Band, formed in 1905, playing at the church fête at Kempsford Manor in 2002.

for the morris men, or those tripping round the maypole, on the village green or in the country house hall for the Servants' Ball, or in the great tithe barn at a harvest home supper. They kept some sort of time for the singers who sang the praises of the Good Lord who bestowed upon them the privilege of working so hard, and the goodness of their master who paid them so little for doing it. The musicians played such an important part in the social life of the village and market town. Yet, their passing on the whole has gone unrecorded and, now, is forgotten. There are a few exceptions and it is to collectors, spearheaded by the great Cecil Sharp, who have given us a small glimpse into the more impromptu, and often self-taught, past activities of the village musician. One name that stands out among the collection is that of John Mason, a farm labourer who was born at Icomb, but at Stow-on-the-Wold when Sharp visited him in 1907-08. From a photograph Sharp took on one of his visits, John Mason smiles serenely – white whiskers framing his face, a soft felt hat on his head, heavy hob-nailed boots on his crippled feet and wearing a well-worn corduroy suit, the knees rucked up above cord ties. Despite his frail physical condition, old John played some forty-six tunes on his fiddle for the famous musician. He died four years later in the Union Workhouse.

Robert Lawrence proudly poses in his Chedworth Band uniform in 1879.

Chedworth seems to have had a long reputation for its musicians, as mentioned by Gibbs, and the present band dates back to its formation in 1905 following the tradition of the old bands before it which were not only brass, but consisted of woodwind and, in some musical groups, strings. The village was fortunate in having skills passed down from one generation to the next by enthusiastic families of musicians. At the turn of the century, the vicar of the time, the Reverend Sacket Hope, had a large family of musicians who organised musical concerts in the schoolroom, encouraging and teaching younger members of the community to take up music. Their efforts were supported and extended by a schoolmaster by the name of 'Ginger Tombs', who made music and singing part of the curriculum in the early 1900s.

An interesting story which is part of the present band's history is that of Albert Allington's bass (an E♭ bass which is a wind instrument). When the young men enlisted in the First World War they were encouraged to take their musical instruments with them. With no motorised transport, marching from place to place was helped along somewhat to the rousing rhythm of a musical march. So Albert took his bass to France in 1915 and was soon after sent up to the front line at Ypres for what they were told would be a couple of weeks. The players left their instruments in a cow shed and covered them with straw for safe keeping until they returned. The couple of weeks stretched into years but, to their surprise and delight, when the few lucky ones returned to the old cow shed there were the instruments, still lying under the straw. Albert's bass was later deposited in the Corinium Museum at Cirencester.

9

THE COTSWOLD YEAR
OF CUSTOMS

New Year begins with more nationally recognised customs, celebrated locally at home with family and friends, or with groups, clubs or societies.

Likewise, Valentine's Day in February and Mother's Day in March are family affairs, so it is at the first major Christian festival of the year that the Cotswolds start their own individual style of celebrations – inherited customs that have stood the test of time and weathered the vagaries of changing social conditions and fashions. Many old traditions, linked to superstitions and country lore, have now largely disappeared; therefore it is only those that are still in existence that are listed in the following calendar.

Palm Sunday, Leafield, near Burford.

In keeping with an ancient tradition the villagers are granted entry at Five Ash Bottom to collect spring water from Wychwood Forest. The spring is reputed to have special medicinal properties. Elsewhere a few churches precede the Morning Service with a procession led by a donkey, and distribute palm crosses to the congregation.

Good Friday

Traditionally the day to plant potatoes and parsley and, of course, to make hot cross buns. Sports now feature alongside church services.

Rogationtide

This was the time for walking the parish boundaries – and this is still done in some places, although the custom of Beating the Bounds now lies more in folklore memory rather than in the unseemly reality suffered by earlier generations, when young boys received a walloping at strategic points en route. This was said to impart in the luckless lads' memories the important points on the boundaries. Kinder communities simply beat a fence or boundary stones with a bundle of twigs. Occasionally one comes across named trees that were planted or marked to identify specific points of geographical significance, or a 'Gospel Oak' or 'St Paul's Epistle' tree, so named from the custom of a reading from the Scriptures being held at that point. Many churches hold special Rogation Day services, and often involves the congregation being invited to walk part of the parish to witness the vicar bless the crops in the surrounding fields.

As with many customs springing from ecclesiastical roots, there was always the chance to turn the occasion into a bit of a jolly. Some places managed to swell the processing congregation very impressively when accompanied by a wagon laden with barrels of local brew and baskets of bread and cheese, and W.E. Adams, writing in his memoirs of the last time the bounds were beaten in the Golden Valley, between Cheltenham and Gloucester, estimated the procession to have reached a total of some two thousand. There was a considerable amount of licensed tomfoolery and no holds were barred to walking the bounds irrespective of any obstacles. This resulted in a conspicuous mansion, called Agg's House, overlooking the town, being entered by 'a deputation from the crowd through one window in the front and out of another at the back' – due to the fact that the house was built over the boundary line of two parishes!

This was in 1845 and as a result of 'a retired tradesman being thrown into the deepest part of the Chelt', and never recovering from the effects, it was the last year that the bounds were beaten at Cheltenham.

Ascension Day

Bisley well-dressing is a colourful affair, instituted in 1863 by the Reverend Thomas Keble (brother of the poet-curate John Keble), taking the idea from the well-dressing at Derbyshire. Schoolchildren, dressed in costume and bearing great circles of flowers, are accompanied by the clergy in a delightful procession through the streets before placing the flowers on Bisley's seven wells.

April

Weekend nearest to the 23rd, Stratford-upon-Avon.

The Shakespeare Birthday Celebrations are a truly English celebration, established for an almost unbroken two centuries to commemorate the country's greatest poet and playwright in the town of his birth. The widely publicised Shakespearian Festival of 1769, organised by the famous David Garrick, laid the foundations for literary pilgrims to beat a path to the birthplace of William Shakespeare, but the present form and character of the celebrations spring from 1824 with a procession through the town to Holy Trinity church, a dinner and some speeches. The tercentenary of Shakespeare's birth in 1864 was marked by a three-week celebration held in a wooden tent, on the opposite side of the Avon from where the theatre stands now. It was in 1879, when the original Shakespeare Memorial Theatre (the predecessor of the present Royal Shakespeare Theatre) was built by Charles Edward Flower, that the first of the annual seasons of Shakespeare's plays was established in Stratford-upon-Avon.

Developed over the years, the focus of the celebrations includes the placing of flowers on Shakespeare's grave as an act of supreme homage, the wearing of rosemary for remembrance, the pulling of flags and banners lining the route of the procession and street entertainment. The Shakespeare Morris Men put the 'Merry' in the Old England atmosphere with their own music and dancing; brass bands, strolling players, circus performers and costumed musicians and children's English folk dancing keep the streets alive in a colourful, joyous medley of music and gentle celebration, redolent of a more leisurely past age.

From its truly local roots, the celebration has grown in stature and standing as an international event. The ceremony of unfurling the flags of nations from all corners of the earth, together with the banners for the works in the Shakespeare canon, signalled by a roll of drums, followed by a commissioned fanfare and the playing of the National Anthem, is a truly moving and spectacular part of the programme. The first invitation to a foreign ambassador, T.F. Bayard from America, was in 1896 and began the now long-established custom of unfurling flags to commemorate those countries that join in the annual public appreciation of Shakespeare. Initially it was the flags of those nations into whose language Shakespeare was in translation, followed by the principle of inviting the world's repre-

Remembered in May – the Levellers at Burford.

prisoners were taken and shut up in the church for three days. On the morning of 17 May the majority were taken up on to the roof of the church to witness the execution of Cornet Thompson, Corporal Church and Private Perkins. An entry in the Parish Register, made by the Vicar after Cromwell's troops and the rest of the prisoners had moved on, recorded that three soldiers had been 'shot to death'. There is now a small memorial plaque on the outside wall of the church commemorating the three soldiers. Another poignant memorial of that violent period in our history is the inscription scratched in the lead of the font: *Anthony Sedley 1649. Prisner.*

Thursday nearest to 12 May, Stow-on-the-Wold, Stow Fair

This is now generally referred to as the Gypsy Fair.

Spring Bank Holiday, Tetbury Wool Sack Races.

Revived in 1973, the custom of running up and down Gumstool Hill carrying a heavy sack of wool dates back to the seventeenth century when the young men of the town thus demonstrated their strength and prowess to impress the young ladies. Gumstool Hill was the main route from Cirencester to Bath and at the foot of the hill was Horsepool Bottom, with its Gumstool (ducking stool). Consequently, this was an area well frequented by travellers, shoppers, traders and a good place in which to show off in front of the ladies of the town. The race is run from the top of the hill, starting outside The Crown Inn, down to The Royal Oak. Races are usually run as a relay, so the sack is dropped and picked up by another runner to return up the hill. For centuries this was an all-male preserve, but now women take part: the weight of the woolsack is 60lb for men, and 35lb for women. The course used to be 320 yards, but was reduced in 1999 to 280 yards when Gumstool Hill was closed to through traffic and the road gated. This is still an impressive test of strength and endurance, considering there is a part of the hill where the incline is 1 in 4, and it attracts a large enthusiastic following each year.

Spring Bank Holiday weekend, Chipping Campden. Robert Dover's 'Cotswold Olimpick Games' on Dover's Hill and Scuttlebrook Wake in the town.

Unique for their place in the history of British country sports and pastimes, Dover's Games have attracted more literary response than any other similar custom. They contain a historical re-enactment of the inauguration of the Games by Robert Dover in 1612 – although, despite many contemporaries writing of Dover 'inventing' or beginning 'the pedigree of Cotswold sports, where each Olimpick game is parraled', Dr Francis Burns, one time Honorary Secretary of the Dover Games Society,

Spring Bank Holiday – Wool Sack Races at Tetbury.

in his MA thesis, gives creditable evidence to suggest that Dover revitalised an already rooted tradition in the Cotswolds.

Whatever their origin, it was Robert Dover, a barrister who settled in the area in 1611, who made the 'Cotswold Olimpicks' in the distinctive form most celebrated over the centuries and formed the nucleus of the present-day festivities. Horse-racing and coursing, jumping, leaping, throwing the sledge-hammer, wrestling, quarter staff fencing and shin-kicking; dancing, and gentler games of skill and chance, kept the North Cotswold hillsides alive with the sounds of contest, music and merry-making. It is generally thought that Shakespeare was one of the notable spectators, and that his line in *The Merry Wives of Windsor* when Slender asks: 'How does your fallow greyhound, Sir? I heard he was out-run on Cotsall' refers directly to the Games at Chipping Campden. There was nothing comparable to them in the whole of the country in the early seventeenth century. The form and scale required, and was given, royal assent by James I, and further support from Charles I until the Civil War. Revived after the Restoration, the Games continued in full swing, as this extract from a notice in the *Gloucester Journal* advertising some of the programme for 1725 shows:

Left and opposite: *Dover's Cotswold 'Olimpicks' at Chipping Campden date back to the reign of James I.*

Dover's Meeting

1819.

The celebrated Sports of this highly distinguished Festival (which have been the Admiration of all honest, learned, and well-disposed Britons for upwards of two Centuries, and which are now patronised and esteemed by all noble, brave, and liberal minded Men, who have a sincere and true regard for their native Country,) will commence as follows :

On THURSDAY in the WHITSUNTIDE WEEK,

UPON THAT HIGHLY ADMIRED AND MOST DELIGHTFUL SPOT

Called,

DOVER'S HILL,

NEAR CHIPPING CAMPDEN, GLOUCESTERSHIRE,

THERE WILL BE A PURSE OF

TWENTY GUINEAS,

To be played for at Backswords,

By Men, as shall be agreed upon, to begin play at three o'clock in the Afternoon ;

TO BE SUCCEEDED BY

Wrestling for a Silver Cup, or three Guineas,

BY NINE MEN ON A SIDE ; ALSO, THERE WILL BE SEVERAL

HANDSOME PRIZES TO BE DANCED FOR,

And excellent Bands of Music will attend ;

LIKEWISE VERY LIBERAL PRIZES WILL BE GIVEN FOR

JINGLING, BOWLING, LEAPING, and RUNNING in SACKS,

Together with a Multiplicity of the Noted Olympic Games and National Sports, peculiar to this ancient Festival, which cannot be detailed in a Bill.

And on FRIDAY, the Sports will commence with a

Horse  Race,

FOR A SWEEPSTAKES OF FIVE GUINEAS EACH, WITH THIRTY-FIVE GUINEAS ADDED THERETO;

For Horses not thorough bred. which have never started against a thorough bred one, or won a Plate. and which have been Hunted the last season, in either of the Counties of *Gloucester, Warwick, Worcester, Oxford, or Hereford* ; to be bona fide the property of the person naming. Four years Old, to carry 10 stone and 5lb. Five years Old, 10 stone and 12lb. Six years Old and Aged, 11 stone and 2lb. the best of Three 2 Miles and a Quarter Heats ; the Horses to be named to the Clerk of the Course, at the House of Mr. ANDREWS, the Old King's Arms Inn, in Chipping Campden aforesaid, on or before Saturday, the 29th day of May preceding the Race, as the Subscription must finally close on that day, for it will be useless to attempt to enter a Horse after the day fixed ; (a Certificate of the Age and Qualification must be produced if required ; three Subscribers or no Race ; all Stakes to be paid to the Clerk of the Course, or to the Steward, by twelve o'clock on the day of running. To be followed by a numberless variety of

The famed Cotswold Sports and Manly Diversions,

NOT EASILY TO BE DESCRIBED.

N. B. The Horses will be started precisely at four o'clock in the Afternoon, and if any dispute arise, the same shall be finally settled by the Steward, (who will be appointed by the Gentlemen of Chipping Campden, at their Meeting, previous to the Race, as usual). All Dogs seen on the Course will be destroyed. No person will be permitted to erect a Booth, or to sell any kind of Liquor or Beverage without previously paying one Guinea to the Conductor of the Sports. A main of Cocks will be fought each Morning in Campden, as usual. Also, excellent Ordinaries, Balls, Plays, and Consorts each day. Tickets for the Steward's Ball, on Friday evening, at the Noel Arms Inn, Ladies' 5s. Gentlemen's 10s. 6d. to be had at the Bar. On Saturday a Wake will be held in Campden, with a variety of Amusements, as usual.

R. ANDREWS, CLERK.

Chipping Campden, April 14th, 1819.

Stratford, Printed at Barnacle's Letter-press and Copper-plate Office, where Engraving is executed in the best stile of Workmanship and Books neatly bound.

> At Dover's Meeting on Campden Hill on Whitson Thursday and Friday
> will be Play'd for as follows:
> The First Day. One Gold Ring and Six Belts to be wrestled for:
> One Lac'd Hat and six pairs of Gloves to be play'd at BackSword for;
> One pair of Mens Shoes and one pair of Womens Lac'd Shoes to be
> danc'd Jiggs for.

Dover himself had set the scene for the ceremonial style of the Games, by presiding over the proceedings regaled in his royal master's cast-off clothes, with ruff and feather hat – acquired for him by his friend and great supporter, Endymion Porter, who was Groom of the Royal Bedchamber for the court of James I. And this is the picture that has become the emblem of the Games. But, despite their auspicious beginnings, the Games invariably attracted the rowdy populace drawn to all such public merry-making, and the condemnation of all such wakes and meetings by their critics. In 1736, a Stow-on-the-Wold minister warned his parishioners in 'A Serious Dissuasive against Whitsun Ales' that 'the evil and pernicious consequences of Whitsun-Ales (namely acts of foolery and buffoonery and relics of paganism such as morris-dances and dancing round the maypole) doth also obtain against Dovers Meetings'.

Threatened by enclosure of the land on which the Games were held at the end of that century, the organisers saved them from extinction by negotiating with the parish of Weston-sub-Edge to hold them on the west side of Kingcomb Lane. By 1818 they had not only found a permanent home, but a respectability bordering on the patriotic, according to a poster of that year:

> The high estimation in which this truly laudable Festival is held (being so famed for the celebrated Olympic Games) is fully evinced by its having been the Admiration of every true and undesigning Briton for more than two centuries, and is now patronised by the Noble Heroes of the present Age…

Meanwhile, while the Games were prey to the parish politics and fashionable sway of the day, diminishing and reviving accordingly, Chipping Campden was still holding its traditional Whit Wake which became known by 1887 as Scuttlebrook Wake, after the Scuttle (or cattle-brook) which at one time ran through the middle of Leysbourne. As with all such activities, world wars imposed their own restrictions, but it was out of the Scuttlebrook Wake that the Games have developed in their present form, thanks to the initiative and formation of the Robert Dover Games Society. The weekend is a spectacular amalgam of pageantry, contests, sports and games, demonstrations and entertainments, music and dancing, with memorable bonfire and firework displays and torchlight procession to make it Cotswold's largest annual jamboree.

First Sunday in May, Randwick, Cheese rolling ceremony

Cheeses are carried to the local church and rolled three times 'widder-shins' (anti-clockwise) round it. This strange custom is but a preliminary to the 'Runnick Wap'.

The following Saturday, Randwick Wap

A contemporary picture of this ancient Mock Mayor-making ceremony was described by a correspondent in the *Gentleman's Magazine* for May 1784:

> As I was last year passing through the village of Randwic, near Stroud, in Gloucestershire, my attention was attracted by a crowd of people assembled round a horse pond, in which I observed a man, on whom I imagined the country people were doing justice in that summary way for which an English mob is famous, though I was the same time surprised to hear them singing, as I thought, a psalm, since I never knew that to be part of the form of such judicial proceedings.
>
> I soon, however, was informed of my error, and learned that it being 2nd Monday after Easter, the people of the parish were assembled, according to an annual custom (the origin of which no one could tell me), to keep a revel. One of the parish is, it seems, on the above-mentioned day, elected mayor, and carried with great state, colours flying, drums beating, men, women, and children shouting, to a particular horse pond, in which his worship is placed, seated in an arm-chair; a song is then given out line by line by the clerk, and sung with great gravity by the surrounding crowd.

The Lord Mayor of Randwic's Song:

When Archelus began to spin,
And Pollo wrought upon a loom,
Our trade to flourish did begin,
Tho' Conscience went to selling broom.
When princes' sons kept sheep in field,
And queens made cakes with oaten flour,
And men to lucre did not yield,
Which brought good cheer to every bower.
But when the giants, huge and high,
Did fight with spears like weavers' beams,
And men in iron beds did lie,

Which brought the poor to hard extremes:
When cedar trees were grown so rife,
And pretty birds did sing on high;
Then weavers lived more void of strife
Than princes of great dignity
Then David with a sling and stone,
Not fearing great Goliath's strength,
He pierc'd his brains, and broke his bones,
Though he was nine feet and a span in length.

Chorus:
Let love and friendship still agree
To hold the bonds of amity.

The instant it is finished the mayor breaks the peace by throwing water in the face of his attendants. Upon this much confusion ensues; his worship's person is, however, considered sacred, and he is generally the only man who escapes being thoroughly souced. The rest of that day, and often of the week, is devoted to riot and drunkenness. The county magistrates have endeavoured, but in vain, to put a stop to this practice. The song was given me by the clerk of the parish, who said it had never been written before. It wants, you observe, some explanation.

The ceremony, with its shades of Feast of Fools, survived for almost another century before its effects were deemed to be so disruptive and disorderly that the church withdrew its support and the Wap finished in 1892. Thanks to the enthusiastic efforts of the then vicar, the late Reverend Niall Morrison, it was revived in 1972 and is still celebrated today, with a few modern innovations such as a Wap Queen, May princesses and cheese bearers adding yet more colour to this ancient and curious custom. It is fitting that its character has been caught so vividly in the memorial window to the much respected and sadly missed Niall Morrison.

Spring Bank Holiday Monday, Cooper's Hill, near Gloucester

At the wake of Cooper's Hill
Each Jack appeared with charming Jill.

Jack and Jill and many hundred others certainly go up the hill, Cooper's Hill, and many of them come tumbling down while running, leaping and rolling to keep their feet on the one-in-one gradient, in the annual Cheese-rolling ceremony. The event has been likened to an annual 'saturnalia' as one theory suggests that villagers were following some pagan ritual of trying to arrest the sun (represented by the cheeses – Double Gloucester, of course) to ensure summer sunlight stayed all year round. Another suggestion has been that in some strange way it is a practice that has lingered from the days when folk carried out extraordinary tests, tasks and feats to establish grazing rights on the common land.

Recalling his childhood memories of the Cooper's Hill Wake, a correspondent to the *Gloucestershire Chronicle* in 1890 penned a detailed picture of some of the characters of the day:

> I can recollect Organ, the master of ceremonies, who was a fine, tall, handsome fellow. He used to appear upon the summit of the hill, dressed in a white linen chemise, adorned with ribbons of all the colours of the rainbow. His hat was also decked with ribbons, and around his waist he wore the belt for which the wrestlers were to struggle, the winner claiming honour as the champion wrestler for the year.
>
> Old Gipsey Jack was always there, with his Asiatic face and his old black fiddle; his wife with eyes like the eagles, a face as brown as a 'bannut' bud and hair as black as a thunder cloud, was there also, with her dingy tambourine; and to the tum-tum of the fiddle and the jingle of the tambourine the country lads and lasses danced to their hearts' content. Organ was the judge of merit in these exercises, and I think the most graceful dancer generally won most of the ribbons. It was a pretty spectacle, and I never witnessed any impropriety. The peasantry were not so learned or so 'refined' as they are now supposed to be; but they were contented and happy.
>
> The grand climax to the annual revel was running down the frightful declivity of the hill after a cheese. It was a perilous feat; but young fellows were ever willing to risk the danger. An old man described the cheese as being 'Hard as Fayrur's heart, or the nether millstone'.

The cheese is now encased in a stout protective container, but the hill has not lost its 'frightful declivity'; neither has the ceremony lost its following and popularity, attracting crowds of spectators and much media interest.

June

Mid-month, Burford, The Dragon Procession

This custom has its roots firmly in the Saxon period, but the earliest history of a settlement at Burford goes back to the Romans, who took advantage of the natural crossing point on the River Windrush. In the year 752 the town was in the Kingdom of Mercia and defended by the

The biennial Open-air Sculpture Show at the Old Rectory in Quenington is recognised as the leading contemporary exhibition of its kind in the UK.

army of King Ethelbad, whose main rival was King Cuthbert of Wessex. In that year the Wessex army advanced on the town and a battle was fought on the ridge to the south west, on what is now Burford Grammar School playing fields and adjacent farmland, over which the busy A40 takes today's traffic. The battle was decisive and the town fell to King Cuthbert. To ensure that the townsfolk were in no doubt as to whom their new masters were, the banner of the Golden Dragon of Wessex was paraded around the town.

For centuries the tradition of processing a painted figure of the victorious dragon around the town on Midsummer Eve was carried on, but eventually died out. The school revived the custom in 1971, and then it was taken over in 1991 by the First Burford Scout Group – it is now their pride and joy. The dragon procession starts at the southern boundary of the town in mid-June each year, as part of the St John the Baptist Patronal Festival. It proceeds down The Hill, through the High Street and into Church Lane to Church Green, where it is greeted by the vicar. However, as the dragon emblem has its roots in pagan mythology, it remains outside the church precincts during the Festal Evensong. The custom has now been integrated into a week-long, wide-ranging programme of musical and other events.

Last Saturday in the month, Northleach Charter Fair

This is a celebration of the town's ancient past and the granting of a Market Charter to the Abbot of Gloucester by Henry III in 1227.

> Henry, King of this realm of England. Greetings!
> Know that we in the sight of God and for the salvation of our soul and the souls of our ancestors and of our heirs have granted by this our charter have confirmed to the Abbot of St Peter's Gloucester and the monks serving God there that they may every year have one fair at the manor of Northleach lasting for three days, namely on the vigil, on the day and the morrow of the apostles Peter and Paul and that they have each week one market on the Wednesday provided that the said fair and the said market are not to the harm of the neighbouring fairs and neighbouring markets. Wherefore we wish and firmly enjoin that the aforesaid abbot and monks shall have and hold the said fair and the said market for ever, well and in peace, freely and quietly with all the privileges and free customs pertaining to them as is aforesaid.
> Witnesses the lords Peter Bish of Winchester
> Joscelin Bishop of Bath
> Robert Bishop of Salisbury
> Hubert De Burgh Earl of Kent
> Ralph Son of Nicholas
> Richard of Agentaine and Henry Capel and others
> Given by the hand of the venerable father Ralph, Bishop of Chichester, our chancellor, at Westminster on the twenty second day of March in the eleventh year of our reign.

It was the Abbot of Gloucester, who owned the land around Northleach from around 780, who built the town next to the medieval village of the Church and Mill End. The weekly market ceased many years ago, but the annual Charter Fair, centred on King George V playing field and in the ancient market place, involves the whole town in its wide-ranging programme of events and attractions.

July

Second weekend, Tewkesbury, Battle of Tewkesbury

This is a re-enactment of the deciding battle of the War of the Roses, including displays of falconry and jousting. The event has grown over the last few years to become one of the largest of its kind in Europe.

August

Second Monday, Cranham Feast

Revived in 1950, this event is essentially a country fair with games and maypole dancing, and a roast – traditionally a deer roasted in the presence of the Lord of the Manor asserting the villagers' rights to the common land.

Bank Holiday Monday, Bourton-on-the-Water, Football in the River

This is not an open competition but an annual match played between two teams organised by the Bourton Rovers Club. The custom is over 100 years old and attracts a huge crowd each year.

Weekend before Bank Holiday, Fairford Steam Rally and Show

This includes arena events, fun fair and a horticultural show. The Rally, started in 1968 (taking the place of the famous pre-war Fairford Carnival), is one of the oldest of its kind in the Cotswolds.

September

Oxford, St Giles' Fair

Dated according to the rhyme below, this ancient fair fills St Giles' and spills over into the adjacent streets – mainly a fun fair appealing 'to children of all ages' with traditional stalls and rides, like the galloping horses, to the hair-raising modern experiences. The following ditty was devised as a 'ready reckoner' by which to work out the date – it is a bit like trying to explain the famous rules of cricket to a foreigner, and likewise, is perfectly logical:

> *Always the first Monday and Tuesday*
> *After the first Sunday in September*
> *Except if 1st September falls on a Sunday.*
> *If Sunday is on 1st September*
> *Then St Giles's is on the following Monday and Tuesday*

About the second weekend, Chipping Norton Mop Fair

Chipping Norton, on the northern spur of the Cotswold hills, is, at 700 feet, the highest town in Oxfordshire. Norton gained its 'Chipping' (market) status as a medieval wool trading centre for the Evenlode Valley. King John granted the town a charter for an annual fair for the sale of wool, and this eventually became a Mop (or Hiring) Fair; now, as with others of the same origin, it is basically a fun fair.

Monday after the first Sunday after 8 September, Witney Feast

Records show that Henry III gave two bucks for the Rector's feast at Witney in 1243, so the origin of what has always been known as Witney Feast really was a feast. Now, it is a large fun fair and, traditionally, an open-air service is held on the Sunday before it opens, the clergy standing among the brightly-painted horses of the old-time roundabout. The old fairs, granted in the thirteenth century, which were more like markets for the business of buying and selling, have long gone from the town's calendar.

Sunday of, or after, 19 September, Painswick Clipping Ceremony

This tradition is part of the old Feast Day, when the congregation of the afternoon church service encircle the parish church of St Mary and sing the special Clipping Hymn. This is a colourful occasion, with many people sporting floral tributes. After the service the traditional Painswick Bun is presented to the vicar and all the children present.

Second Saturday, Gloucester, Barton Fair

October

October is the month for the old Mop Fairs, now all Fun Fairs, at Cirencester, Moreton-in-Marsh, Stratford-upon-Avon, Tewkesbury, Winchcombe and Woodstock

Thursday nearest to 24 October, Stow (Gypsy) Fair

November and December

Second Thursday, Northleach, public meeting of the ancient Court Leet

The Court Leet is as old as the town, and this is one of the few places left in the whole of the country to carry on the custom of meeting annually to appoint the law enforcement officers (now honorary positions), under the presidency of the Lord of the Leet – a hereditary office held by the Lord Bathurst of Cirencester 'from time immemorial'. The Leet is the

Ploughing championships and country fairs mark the start of autumn, and displays of skill in traditional horse-drawn methods attract an enthusiastic following.

earliest form of democracy in local government, before town and parish councils were formed, and the delegation of responsibilities rests with the officials. The Lord, as undisputed and acknowledged authority, needs no badge of office, and he appoints his High Steward. The High Bailiff is elected each year by a jury of twelve men for a period of one year. The two Constables have their staves, and the town mace is on show as the insignia of the Court Leet. The ancient offices of Hayward to look after the town's common lands, and the Tithing Men whose responsibilities are for the town boundaries, are still upheld as in medieval times, together with the interesting post held by two Ale-tasters, called Carnal, who are instructed to taste the ale before offering it to the Lord. The major collective role of the Leet is as trustee of all the charities in the town, with some seventy to eighty acres of common land and eight almshouses to administer as well as looking after the old Hundred of Cirencester. On completion of the annual Court business, a large body (males only) retire to the old Cotswold Hall for a five-course meal. The evening's duties are only deemed as being completed after all the toasts to crown and country, including clerics and services, have been gone through – amounting to some thirteen speeches with their thirteen replies.

Advent

The four weeks leading up to Christmas have become a time to 'Light Up', following the previous Sunday becoming known as 'Stir Up Sunday' – traditionally the latest date for making the Christmas pudding if it is to mature in time for the great day. Advent markets have now become a major feature throughout the Cotswolds, usually combined with lighting up the streets with sparkling decorations and switching on the lights of the parochial Christmas tree. Small fairgrounds, street entertainment, mulled hot drinks, bands and buskers, stalls and stilt-walkers, maybe a sleigh or carriage ride, morris dancing and mumming, carol-singing and the ubiquitous Father Christmas are all, or in part, to be found at the Advent markets. Bourton-on-the-Water, pretty and popular in all seasons, is a magical village at this time with its Christmas tree set in the river, its lights reflecting shafts and stars of shimmering colour into the water, thanks to the efforts of the town's Chamber of Commerce. The tradition of setting the tree in the river between the small bridges, which give the village the nickname of Little Venice, has been established for at least a quarter of a century.

Christmas-tide

Carol concerts, mummers' plays, Nativity plays, local Christmas bazaars and the perennial pantomime - there is something going on somewhere

Christmas time is Panto time in village halls throughout the Cotswolds, keeping the community spirit and tradition alive, as here at Avening.

at some time over this period. It is always worth looking out for the small handwritten notice in the village shop or pub or in a church porch to see the true Cotsaller at home as well as the wider advertised professional entertainments.

Boxing Day

This is the traditional day for the County Hunt Meet – the one at Cirencester Park is particularly popular.

The City of Gloucester Mummers perform at mid-day outside the Cathedral on this day.

In Bibury there is the the annual Duck Race, organised by Bibury Cricket Club, which attracts hundreds of spectators and 'punters' urging on the yellow plastic ducks as they bob their way along the trout-filled water of the River Coln while raising substantial funds for charities.

New Year's Eve

It is customary for the local bell-ringers to ring out the old year for half an hour before midnight, then ring in the new as soon as the church clock strikes twelve. Many places now welcome in the New Year with local firework displays and private parties.

A Cotswold Glossary

A

A babbled: he (or she) spoke in a
rambling fashion. Shakespeare used it
liberally in *Henry V* in Mistress
Quickly's poignant telling of Falstaff's
passing: 'and a babbled of green
fields'.

Abear: tolerate. 'I can't abear that kind
of talk'

Above a bit: a bit more than. 'He was
above a bit of six foot'

According: in relation to. 'He is a bright
boy according to his age'

Acquaintance: sweetheart

Adam's ale: water

Addled: confused

Adone: have done (with it)

Adry: thirsty

Afeared: frightened

After: alongside – 'The river runs after
the road'

Afterclaps: consequences, but only if
something disagreeable results

Agen: against. Also denotes 'by the time'
– 'It'll be ready agen you're back
home'

Agree with: put up with

Ails: the beards of barley

Aim: to try

Ajorum: a lot (usually of food)

Anearst and anighst: near

Arged: argued

Aron: ever a one

Ashen: ash tree

Asum or Ashum: Evesham

Asum jasum: spick and span

Avore: before

Away with: put up with

Axed: asked

Ay-gras: pasture land that has not been grazed for years

B

Bachelor buttons: scabious

Backend: usually refers to autumn – 'we tidy up the garden at the backend'

Bannut: walnut

Barm: yeast

Barton: farm yard

Beestings: first milk after cow has calved (also known as cherry curds)

Beggars: puzzles; worries – 'that really beggars me'

Besom: broom

Best: superior – 'he could best me at running'

Bide: to stay – 'she was willing to bide awhile'

Blind worm: slow worm

Blow: blossom – 'the fruit trees were all a blow in the Ashum Vale'

Blusterous: boisterous

Boss: tuft

Boughten: shop bought, to distinguish from home made

Brave: in good health – 'I was fair to middlin', but be brave enow now'

Breeds: the brim (of a hat) or the forecast (in connection with weather) – 'the cows are lying down and that breeds fine'

Briched: of wealth – 'they came from a well-briched family'

Brit: over-ripe corn

Bumby in the game of Bandy: Bandy was an old Cotswold game resembling hockey. A crooked stick was cut from the hedgerow and a ball made from a roughly shaped block of wood, called a nunney. There were very few rules except that a player could not obstruct the nunney with his body while the nunney was hit from hedge to hedge in narrow country lanes, or small enclosed yards. Only the stick was allowed to intercept. If a player put his foot out to stop the nunney then the opposition shouted *Turn Bumby*; to fail to do so immediately gave them licence to set about the offending Bumby.

Burr: sticky seed pod

Burra (burrow): shelter or lee side – 'the sheep got in the burra out of the wind'

Butter leaves: leaves of the Striplex hortensis, grown for dairymaids to wrap round butter pats for market

C

Caddle: awkward business – 'it was a real caddle to get there'

Cant: gossip

Canting shop: house known for being a centre of gossip

Capper: head

Casual: inclement (of weather)

Cawkey: touchy

Charm: birdsong – 'the charm in my garden at dawn is a wonder to behold'

Chestle money: Roman coins found in the county of Gloucestershire. The term usually refers just to brass coins

Child: a female infant – 'Mercy on's, a barne; a very pretty barne! A boy or a child, I wonder' (*A Winter's Tale*)

Chizzomed: sprouted – first shoots after a tree, shrub or plant has been pruned

Chunny: house sparrow

Chur or chore: small alleyway between houses

Church pigs: woodlice

Chure: opening, but only when referring to an entry to house or passageway

Churchyard cough: particularly loud, hacking and persistent cough

Clack: noise

Claggy: muddy, but particularly in relation to the soil of the garden

Clavey: mantelpiece

Comical: awkward, but of a person – ''ee be a right comical chap when 'eed a mind'

Cooch: tough grass, quick to grow and slow to burn

Cow leech: cattle doctor

Coxy: restive

Crib: cottage – 'they've got a nice little crib down by the mill'

Cripped or crimped: tightly curled hair

Crowdy: pig's head broth

Crutch or cratch: a thatcher's stick with a V end, used for carrying the 'yealms' or 'helms' (bundles) of straw

Cullins: poultry feed, the smallest grains winnowed out from corn

Cuppie hens: chickens

Cut: drunk – 'he was three parts cut'; also amusing – 'he looked a proper cut in that hat'

Cyaw: to stare around in a nosy fashion

D

Dabster: a cunning fellow

Daddocky: unsafe (usually referring to decaying wood) – 'those steps are old, they seem a bit daddocky'

Dang (or dall) my rags: a mild curse meaning 'Damn me if…'

Dap: bounce – 'we used to dap the ball against the wall'; can also refer to a person behaving spryly – 'she would dap along smartish for her age'

De-de: secretive – 'they were talking very de-de in the corner'

Dedious: deep conversation

Devil in a bush: *Nigella damascena*

Dibber: setting pin, short wooden pointed tool for making holes in the garden for planting

Dight: a proud thing – 'she was dight of a body'

Dimpsy: twilight

Docksy: over-dressed woman

Dot: jot – 'I'll dot it down quick before I forget'

Dough kiver: bread-making trough

Dout: to extinguish a light

Drawed out: dressed up – 'she was really drawed out for the wedding'

Dree: three

Drock: open ditch

Drock-mouthed: said of a ewe losing her teeth

Dryth: dryness – 'there's no dryth in the weather'

Dub: throw – 'they would dub at them apples till they got one to fall'

Duff: baked suet pudding

Dummel: drowsy, used of wasps and bees in a sleepy state at the end of summer

Dump: boiled pudding

Dunch: plain

Dunch dunny: stupid, dull, deaf

Dunnekin: privy, outside primitive toilet

Durgan: the smallest horse in a plough team

Dyow bit (dew-bite): the first food taken in the morning, but not as substantial as breakfast

E

Ean: to produce lambs

Eckle: green woodpecker

Eddish: newly-cut stubble of corn

Edge on: eager for

Eenastwur: even as it were

Eever grass: tussock

Eevy: dampness of walls or stone flag-
stones signifying rain or 'heavy'
weather

Egg-pegs: *Prunus spinosa*

Ellern: elder tree

Ellum: elm tree

Elmen: made of elm wood

Em: them

Emmet: ant

Enent: opposite

Enewst: much the same

Enow: enough

Enteny: main door of house

Evet: newt

Eye: to look over; also a brood of
pheasants

F

Faggot: used for a mischievous child or a
wily old woman

Fammel: hungry, famished

Feature: resemble – 'I don't think my son
does feature me'

Felt: a fieldfare

Feneague: cheat – 'you have to watch her,
she's been known to feneague at
cards'

Feggy dump: plum pudding – usually
refers to Christmas pudding

Fetched out: dressed up – ''Er was all
fetched out in a new hat'

Few: many – 'there were a good few at
the church fête'

Field: denotes a ploughed field rather
than pasture land

Filler: the shaft horse

Fills: the shafts of a wagon or cart

Firm asleep: used to denote a deep sleep
in place of the phrase 'fast asleep'

First: used at the end of a sentence
instead of such explanations as to why,
for instance – 'he couldn't get there
on time, but he won't be long first';
also used instead of rather, again at
the end of a sentence – 'she said she
would keep them first'

Fistle: to fidget about

Fit: feet, but only when referring to
humans or animals. For measurements
the singular 'foot' is used – 'he was a
tall man, over six foot'

Fitchet: a ferret

Flear: the lacy fat membrane from a pig
rendered down to make lard

Flickets: potatoes

Flirt: flutter

Flisk: a brief shower

Flitch: side of bacon

Flummoxed: muddled, bewildered

Foreright: directly opposite to

Fossicking: fussing

Fought: fetched

Fousty: musty – 'you can't use that flour
now, it's gone fousty'

Frail: workman's rush basket for carrying
his food

Freddy: a tramp

Freeman's walk: a free tea

Frigary: a difficult situation

Frum: firm, also luxuriant (of growth)

G

Gad-about: a kind of child's support on
castors to aid walking

Gadling: an idle fellow

Gaitle: to wander aimlessly

Galligantus: used to describe an animal of
very much larger size than normal

Gallus: impudent

Gallytraps: ostentatious ornaments of dress

Garn: garden

Gawk: to gape or stare

Gibberwauling: derisory term for monotonous out of tune singing

Gid: gave

Gilliflower: wallflower

Gimmals: hinges

Girt: great

Gleany: guinea fowl

Glim: a soft light

Glouty: surly

Goat owl: nightjar

Goggle: giddy

Goggle-headed: top heavy

Gony: a simple-minded person

Goosegrass: (also known as 'sweethearts') the sticky creeping weed *Galium aparine*

Griggly: feeling of squeamishness when told something unpleasant

Grime: the black smut on a fire grate

Griz: to grind the teeth

Grizbite: to gnash the teeth

Gulkin: a small dell with a stream at the bottom

Gullocks: to gulp greedily

H

Hackle: to make an awkward job of something – 'he made a right hackle of it'

Haddlin: the headland of a field where the plough could not reach

Half named: privately baptised

Half-saved: half-witted

Ham: level meadowland pasture

Hameleets: cloth buskins or strips bound round the legs to protect the legs of farm workers in the wet fields

Hames: the support of a horse's collar that holds the traces

Handing post: sign post

Handy: near to – 'the house is handy to the shops'

Haulms: stalks of pulse crops such as beans, and of corn

Hawsens: hawthorn berries

Hawzen: chide, scold

Hedgepegs: sloe berries

Hedge pig: hedgehog

Heel: the top crust of a loaf of bread

Hern: hers

Hether: the top bindings of a laid hedge

Hikey: stuck up – 'she was proper hikey when she left the village'

Hiring money: the shilling that was paid at the old Mop Fairs forming the contract of the employer hiring the servant for a year

Hitched: married

Harbour: encourage or shelter – 'if you keep the corn in the shed it will harbour mice'

Hindersome: hindering

Hob: the third swarm of bees

Hobbedy's lantern: Will o' the wisp

Hobbledehoy: a tramp

Hobblionkers: the game of 'conkers' played with horse chestnuts

Hocksey: of weather, drizzly enough to make roads slippery

Hockshet: a hogshead – a measure of cider of about a hundred gallons

Hodmadod: a snail

Hoggish: stubborn

Hollow: the whine of the wind when it 'boards' (foretells) rain

Holywake: bonfire (from the burning of heretics)

Hop-about: apple dumpling

Horrocks: a very large fat woman – 'she
    be a horrocks of a 'ooman'
Horsenest: a well-worn tale often told
Hot: to heat up – 'He'd only got to hot
    it up'
Hote: a rabbit's burrow
Housen: houses
Hove: swelling
Howgy: huge
Howsomever: however
Huck: to bargain
Huck muck: dwarfish in stature
Hud: shell or outer husk
Huff: of pastry which is very light, but not
    quite the same texture of puff pastry
Hummel: to dress barley
Hummer: a mischievous child
Hummock: a mound of earth
Hurd: a corruption of 'hoard', to store up

Note: the H is so often omitted,
the legendary Gloucestershire
cricketer, Dr W.G. Grace, should
be accorded his place in the annals
of our local lore by famously
appealing so often: 'I never 'it it'.

I

Idraphobies: depression – 'he'd really got
    the idraphobies and wouldn't smile at
    anything'
Iffing and Aahing: deliberating, being
    indecisive
Inch-meal: by inches, all over
Ivy flower: anemone

J

Jack and his team: the Great Bear
    constellation known as The Plough
Jack Hern: a heron

Jack Leg knife: a clasp knife
Jadder: a stone cutter
Jeremy Diddler: an up-to-no-good
    simpleton
Jerry house: a beer house
Jibbols: small spring onions, not fully
    formed
Jobbing lot: an assortment of items sold
    together
Joggle: to jolt and shake about
Jolly: a fool
Jommetry: a muddled mess – ''tis all of a
    jommetry'
Jonnock: the truth – 'she told me herself,
    so I know it's jonnock'
Jopple: a small job, a trifling task
Junk: a tasty stew or hash
Justers: weighing scales

K

Keck: tickly cough – 'I've done nothing
    but keck all day'
Kid: pod, but only when growing
    – 'those beans haven't come into kid
    yet'
Kidney beans: runner beans
King: used as a comparative term to
    indicate an enormous improvement
    – 'I be a king to what I was last week'
Kipe: a rush basket holding 70lb of
    potatoes; often that amount was
    referred to as 'a kipe of taters'
Kiss behind the garden gate: *Saxifraga
    umbrosa*
Kive: tub used for fermenting home-
    made wines and ales
Knap: a knoll of land
Knit-bone: comfrey
Knowed: knew

L

Lady's mantle: *Alchemilla vulgaris*

Lagger: narrow copse or spinney alongside a field

Langet: a long strip of land, this often appears in place names

Lapstone: a cobbler's pebble used to welt the leather on to the shoe. It got its name from always being on the cobbler's lap in readiness

Larrop: flog, beat 'if I catch him I'll gi'ee a good larroping'

Lay: pasture land

Leaf: means the same as flear, the lacy fat membrane from a pig rendered down to make lard

Leaping stock: mounting block built against the wall of a stable or building (many inns still have them) to aid the rider to mount a big horse

Learn: teach. This survived in written form until the seventeenth century. Shakespeare uses it in *Two Gentlemen of Verona* – 'A thousand more mischances than this one have learned me how to brook this patiently'

Leastways: anyway

Leathern bat: common bat

Leaze or leese: to glean the fallen ears of corn after harvest, an ancient rite dating back to biblical times. Dryden explains it: 'She in harvest used to leese, But harvest done, to chare-work did aspire'

Lections: intentions

Leer: a feeling of being unwell through hunger – 'I'd bin out all day wi'out any vittals an' were quite leer by the time I got whoam'

Lennow: to make pliable – 'you need to lennow it first'

Lent grain: spring crops

Lestest: least

Levence: dough set to ferment

Lewarm: lukewarm

Lick: to beat, in a competitive sense – 'Our Ern could lick him at bowls any day'

Licker: a mystery, puzzle – ''tis a licker as how 'tis done'

Likely: promising

Lippet: a shred – ''twas torn to a lippet'

Loppit: a trollop

Lowry: low-lying cloud – ''tis a bit lowry yonder, boards rain, wouldn't wonder'

Lug: a measure of land, a perch

M

Maid: a young girl. Maids (servants) were referred to as girls

Malkin: a mop made of rags

Mammer: to bewilder by repetition – ''ee would keep on over and over till me poor yud was that mammered'

Mander: to scold

Marriage lines: marriage certificate

Mathen: wild ox-eyed daisy

Maundy: cheeky

Mawkin: a scarecrow

Mazards: small black cherries

Meg: a trifling sum

Mere: a balk of land dividing one field or patch from another, still to be found in field names

Messengers: small clouds detached from larger ones, betokening rain

Midden: dunghill

Middling: used to describe a state of health. 'Pretty middling' – quite well; 'middling' – pretty well; 'fair to middling' – in a poor state; 'very middling' – not much hope!

Leazing (or gleaning), *c.* 1890.

Miles endways: long miles

Millerd: a miller

Minskin: the household rubbish pit

Misword: disagreement

Mizzle: light rain

Moithered: unable to think clearly

Moleshag: a grub that eats cabbage plants

Mollicrush: to pulp into jelly

Molly: a man doing housework, or whatever used to be generally regarded as women's work around the house

Moot: stump of tree or shrub

Mop: hiring fair

Mort: a large quantity – 'he'd had a mort to drink that night'

Mortal: very – 'I was mortal glad when he'd finished'

Mortify: to tease – 'he was a dabster at mortifying the girls'

Mousen: mice

Muckinger: an old rag used instead of a handkerchief

Mugglement: confusion, muddle

Mullocks: a large cock of hay; a heavy fall – 'he slipped on the mud, went a real purler and fell a mullock'

Mumruffians: chaffinches

Must: the sediment of crushed apples and pears after pressing for cider or perry

N

Nail bit: a gimlet

Nale: alehouse

Nation: extremely – 'he was nation worried about his job'

Natomy: a skinny person

Neddy: a foolish, dull person (likening

them to a donkey)

Neglection: neglect

Nern: never a one – 'I was nern to gossip idly'

Nesh: weak, delicate – 'these plants are a bit nesh as yet'

Nesses: nests

Nineter: an artful lad

Ninny: a foolish person

Ninte: treat with ointment – 'Shep did ninte those two ewes agin the scab'

Nither: shrammed with cold – 'she came in all of a nither'

No-aways: never

Nobbut: none but only – 'there's nobbut like my father'

No good on: good for nothing

Not: a kind of hockey played with hedgerow sticks

Notable: industrious

Numman idles: pansies (probably a corruption of Love-in-idleness)

Nuncheon: luncheon

O

Obligated: obliged

Obstrapulous: obstreperous

Oddsies: remainder

Odmedod: someone who is not all they seem – 'she was a bit of an odmedod for all her fancy ways'

Oinions (pronounced 'oyneuns'): onions

Old maid: horsefly

Onaccountable: extremely

Oodle: pronunciation of 'wood-wail', the nightingale

Ooman: woman

Oonderment: an object of wonder, also used for some form of trickery – 'he was up to his oonderments again'

Oont: mole

Oontitump: molehill

Oose: hose

Oot: will you, derived from 'wilt thou' – 'come yere, oot?'

Oozeling: wheezing

Ope: opening

Orts: leftovers

Otheren: other

Otherous: otherwise, different

Ourn: ours

Outasked: the third time of calling banns of marriage – 'they were outasked last Sunday'

Outride: commercial traveller

Overget: to recover from an illness (transposition of 'get over')

Overent: opposite, against something

Owlas: idle in an indifferent sort of way

Owless: lazy in a careless, thoughtless manner

Owt: strength or substance – 'there was no owt in that last brewing'

P

Paired: mouldy, of cheese

Pan: a pond

Pargeter: a plasterer

Pawk: to be out of breath

Peart: lively and perky

Peck: pickaxe

Peckied or pickied: something ending in a pointed end, usually referring to the shape of a garden or plot of land

Peck-shaft: handle of a pickaxe

Peep: dawn light – 'I was up this morning just as it was about to peep'

Pelf: weeds

Pen: hill

Peth: crumbly bread – ''twas all of a peth when I cut that other loaf'

Pifkin: a small jug (pronunciation of

'pipkin' as used by Beatrix Potter in *The Tailor of Gloucester*)

Pig-meat: pork, fresh from a newly-killed pig

Pigscote: pigsty

Pinnikin: fastidious

Pip: a bud or young shoot

Pitch: the amount picked up at a time on a hay-fork

Plant: a crop – 'thirty acres always gave a good plant of barley'

Plash: a small pool, usually used in context of a village street stream

Pleach: intertwining of branches, used in hedge-laying or in a garden bower

Plim: swell – 'if you soak the raisins in cold tea they'll plim up nice and juicy'

Plunt: large, knobbly walking stick

Plushes: the bands tying the heather or sticks on a besom

Pollards: a mixture of peas and beans grown in the same plot

Pootchin: a coarse apron with a large pocket used for carrying seed for sowing

Polting lug: a long pole used in orchards to knock the fruit from the high branches

Posset: bread soaked in beer. Later it became the name of a concoction of whipped egg white and cream with wine

Pot: a quantity of fruit – 100lb of pears; 90lb of plums; 84lb of apples

Povey: owl

Puckfoust: puffball fungus

Puddle: to work slowly

Pugs: the short quills left in the skin of a fowl when plucked

Punishment: pain

Pur-lamb: the survivor of twin lambs

Purler: a heavy fall

Q

Quag: quagmire

Quakers: quaking grass

Quar: stone quarry, also to cut – 'they would have to quar more stone to finish the job'

Quat: squat, crouch

Queer Street: in trouble, usually applied to getting into debt – 'I told her that if she didn't cut the coat according to the cloth, they'd all end up in Queer Street'

Quest: the cry of a dog on the scent – 'the hounds were in full quest'

Quib: to query or argue – 'he would quib about the smallest thing'

Quicken tree: mountain ash

Quilt: to swallow – 'my throat was that bad I could hardly quilt'; 'the tale he told me was so far-fetched I could scarcely quilt it'

Quist: wild ring dove

Quitch: cooch grass

Quod: prison – 'he was given seven days in quod for vagrancy'

Quodlins: coddling apples

R

Rabble: a road worker who shovelled the edges to clear the rubbish

Raisty: rancid – 'is that bacon alright, seems a bit raisty to me'

Ramp: rage, but usually only associated with pain – 'I had ramping toothache all night'

Rantipole: a particularly noisy, boisterous child

Rathe: early crop, usually of fruit

Road 'rabbles'.

Rattletraps: derogatory term for useless articles

Reeving string: a drawstring in a garment

Rest part: the remainder

Rime: hoar frost

Rivel: wriggle – 'he would rivel up his nose if you mentioned cabbage'

Robin Redbreast pincushion: the hairy red gall on the wild rose

Rook together: to huddle up

Rookery: a jumble of articles

Round: to lie in bed between, say, 10 p.m. and 10 a.m. (from 'round the clock')

Rove: to dry meat by smoking

Rubber: whetstone for sharpening a scythe

Ruffet: rough grass

Running: rennet – 'that cheese will need more running to set it'

Runnock: the youngest child of the family, or the smallest pig in a litter

S

Sally: the willow

Scantity: scarce

Scawt: to hurry along in a flustered state. Also to work hard – 'I had a scawt all day to get done'

Scholard: scholar

Scrag: a branch of a tree that is forked but crooked

Scratchlings: the scrumpy bits left in the pan after lard has been rendered down. These were great treats served on bread, liberally salted, at pig-killing time

Scrawling: a light frost

Scrump: to crunch up, usually by stepping heavily on something; steal (apples)

Shard: a broken gap in a fence

Shepster: starling, from its characteristic settling on a sheep's back

Ship: sheep

Shrammed: feel chilled to the bone

Staddle stones support the thatched cricket pavilion at Stanway, keeping it above the flood plain of the field.

Skag: a tear as opposed to a cut – 'be careful not to skag that jacket when blackberrying'

Skiddy: the wren

Skimmer Lad: a dumpling dough lid on top of the cooking pot; it used to be made on the skimmer, hence its name

Slack: very small bits of coal used to 'bank' up the fire

Slammerkin: slovenly

Slat: a stone slate (roofing tile)

Sleight: the area where sheep are fenced (rather than penned) after coming from pasture

Slicker: curds and whey in cheesemaking

Smalter: small beer

Snowl: a hunk of bread, but usually associated with taking it to work rather than a piece served at the table – 'I'd just set down to eat my snowl and cheese when Carter sed it was time to get back to the 'osses'

Souring: vinegar

Sparrow grass: asparagus

Speeds: the dried particles from the tear ducts of the eye

Sprack: lively

Spreathed: rough and sore chapped skin, usually as a result of not drying hands etc. thoroughly before going out into the cold wind

Staddle: the stone mushroom-shaped top supporting the flat base upon which ricks were built. Rats and mice were defeated by the flat undersides of the 'mushroom'

Stag: a 'stroller' potato, one that has been left in the ground from the previous year's harvest and produces a small crop the following season

Stagger Bob: a newly-born calf

Stank: a dam of natural weeds and sticks in a river, as opposed to a built-up barrier

Stew: a small pond of fish, referred to in old manuscripts, particularly relating to monastic fish ponds

Stwan or stwon: stone

Swill: wash – 'I've just got to swill these few things out'

T

Tabling: the coping of a gable end or wall

Tallet: a hay loft or floor over a barn reached by outside stone steps

Tally: twenty-five sacks of corn

Tantadlin: apple dumpling

Teart: painful

Teel: to pile up

Terrify: irritate, usually refers to flies worrying cattle

Tester: sixpence

Tetter: a blister, usually refers to one on the tongue

Think on: to recall – 'I can't think on that incident you refer to'

Thissum: this

Tiddle: fidget

Tiddliwick: beer house

Tiddlin: the weakest puppy in the litter, or a lamb brought up by hand

Timbersome: very weighty

Tisty tosty: a ball made from the heads of cowslips

Tommy: bread

Tommy-bag: lunch bag

Took to: taken aback – 'well, when he said that I was proper took to'

Tote: the whole thing

Trumpery: garden rubbish, but only of plant and shrub debris

Tush: the wing of a ploughshare

Tuzzy muzzy: Old man's beard, *Clematis vitalba*; also a burr, usually of the burdock

A tallet at Chedworth.

U

Un: him or it

Undrements: pranks

Unket: lonely, dull in spirit

Unsuity: not of a regular pattern

Upon times: occasionally – 'I get lonely
   upon times'

Upping block: mounting block

Upshard: stop gap

Urchin: hedgehog

V

Vails: perks (perquisites) – 'the leazers
   used to pick up all the loose corn
   they could hold in their aprons at the
   end of the harvest, that was their vails'

Vapoured: hitting out in a threatening
   manner, usually confined to swiping
   out at a wasp; an Avening wheel-
   wright, speaking about his part in the
   village Mummers' play at the turn of
   the century said of his fight with the
   Black Knight: 'we vapoured about
   with our swords'. The word was an
   everyday expression around 1650,
   meaning to fool about, to show off, or
   to swagger.

Varges: verjuice, to denote something
   extremely sour – ''twas as sour as
   varges'

Vaz out: to become frayed at the edges

Vaze: to shuffle about aimlessly

Vazzelement: a tangle

Verment: vermin, also means savage

Viper's dance: St Vitus's dance

Vittals: food

Vlobber: to talk stupidly

Vocate: to ramble meaninglessly

W

Wall pepper: *Sedum acre*

Waps: wasp

Wash-dish: the water wagtail

Water bubbles: kingcups

Watty handed: left-handed

Wavewind: bindweed

Well gated: busy, plenty to do

Well up: eminent – 'his son was well up
   in medicine'

We'm: we are

Wet: rain – come in out of the wet

Whiffle: the sound of wind moaning in
   a chimney

Whirligig: a turnstile

Whosen: whose

Wickering: the neighing of a horse

Wickers: a horse's ears

Will Jill: an effeminate kind of man

Wimble wamble: unsteady walk

Wimwam: an extraordinary contrivance
   that is beyond the person's powers of
   description

Winter stuff: winter greens

Wisp: a stye on the eyelid

Witchify: bewitch

Wood sprite: green woodpecker

Woppered: worn out, fatigued

Worrit: an aggravating person – 'he's a
   proper little worrit when he's a mind'

One peculiarity of the Cotswold
dialect is that W is usually ignored
completely if it is followed by an
O – becoming double O instead.
Thus, woman becomes ooman,
but in the plural the W is used, as
in women – this is due entirely
to the different sounds of the O
in woman (ooh) but the O in
women is sounded as 'wimmen'.

If, however, the W is followed by a double O then the consonant is given, even when two words used together sound the same but are spelt differently. For example, 'would' and 'wood': 'She ood go to the wood pile'. An almost melodic phrase is 'ah uh ood' for 'Yes she (or he) would'!

Y

Yan: the first lamb

Yapper: to talk

Yappermag: a gossip

Yappern: apron

Yarbs: herbs

Yare: pronunciation of hair and hare. An excellent example of Yud (head) and Yare (hair) appears in the old ballad called 'George Ridler's Oven':

The sturuns that built George Ridler's oven
They kwum from Blakeney's quar
And George he wur a jolly ol' mon
And his yud it grow'd above 'is yare

Yealm: a bundle of straw for thatching

Yean: to lamb

Yellocks: a transposition of an exclamation 'look ye'

Yeows: ewes

Yorks: leather bands tied or buckled round cord breeches just below the knee of farm workers. The old men said it was to stop the mice running up their trouser legs, particularly during threshing. It was a handy place to tuck in the little 'dibbing' knife, or a short-bladed knife, to have handy for scraping their tools as they worked – especially useful in the garden

You'm: you are

Yourn: yours

Yunt: is not, when used as a direct negative – 'No, it yunt near Thursday'

Yur: here

Z

Z is mostly used as a harsher sibilant of S, as in 'zum zays zo' for 'some says so'.

Zong of Zaint Zwithin's Day (see Folksongs chapter) is a fine example of this.

BIBLIOGRAPHY

Primary Sources

Chronicle of Robert of Gloucester

Cotswold Characters by Cotswold Tape Recording Society: Miss Amy Cook of
  Wotton-under-Edge, interviewed by Peter Duddridge

County Record Office, Gloucester (Basket Penny Toll, Ref: Tetbury Feoffees' Records,
  document number D566 B14)

Dursley Workhouse Committee Report (extract) 1839

English Place Names Society

Queen's College, Oxford University Archives

Vaughan Williams Library, Cecil Sharp House

Secondary Sources

Bayly, Thomas Haynes: *The Mistletoe Bough* (Thomas Haynes Bayly 1797-1839)

Bullock, Donald: *The Legend that was Clapham* (Wheatley Press 2002)

Burns, Dr Francis: *Heigh for Cotswold* (date unknown)

Davey-Smith, A.B.: *Nailsworth 1500-1900* (pub *Stroud News and Journal* – undated)

Denning, Anthony (revised by Paul Ranger): Theatre in the Cotswolds (pub The
  Society for Theatre Research 1993)

Evans, Herbert A: *Highways and Byways of Oxford and the Cotswolds* (Macmillan 1905)

Gibbs, J Arthur: *A Cotswold Village* (John Murray 5th edition 1903)

Gloucestershire Village Book, The: Gloucestershire Federation of Women's Institutes (pub jointly with Countryside Nooks 1987)

Lewis, June R: *Cotswold Villages* (Robert Hale 1974)

— *Walking the Cotswold Way* (David and Charles 1986)

— *Cotswold Cook Book* (Cotswold Life 1990)

— *The Village School* (Robert Hale 1989)

— *The Secret Diary of Sarah Thomas* (Windrush Press 1994)

— *The Cotswolds: Life and Traditions* (Weidenfeld and Nicolson 1996)

— *A History of Farmor's School* (Hendon Publishing 1982)

— *A History of Fairford* (Hendon Publishing 1982)

— *Cotswolds at War* (Alan Sutton 1992)

— *The Witch's Mark* (Robert Hale 1973)

— *Handbook of Crafts and Craftsmen* (Robert Hale 1978)

plus material from other features to AA Leisure Series books and BBC Radio talks,
McCormick, Donald: *Murder by Witchcraft* (London 1968)

Meredith, Bob: *The Haunted Cotswolds* (Reardon 1990)

Moody, Raymond and Joan: *The Book of Burford* (Barracuda Books 1983)

Palmer, Roy: *Folklore of Gloucestershire* (Tempus Publishing ed 2001)

Potter, Beatrix: *The Tailor of Gloucester* (Frederick Warne 1901)

Rolt, LTC: *Worcestershire* (pub Robert Hale 1949)

Rudge, Thomas: *Fairs and Weekly Markets in Gloucestershire 1807* (1807)

Smyth, John: *Berkeley Manuscripts*

Stawell, Jessica: *Aldsworth 1000-2000* (Aldsworth 2000)

The History of Tetbury Society: *Tetbury, The Place and People* (2001)

Verey. David: *Gloucestershire, The Cotswolds* (Penguin 1970)

Victoria History of the County of Gloucester, The: Vol VII, published by Oxford University
Press

Williams, Adin: *Lays and Legends of Gloucestershire* (C.H. Savory Steam Press, Cirencester
– undated)

Periodicals

Cotswold Life magazine (various)

Gloucestershire and Avon Life (various)

Gloucestershire Countryside (various) 1931-1942

Gloucestershire Echo (various)

Gloucester Journal (various)

Jackson's Oxford Journal (various) 1753-1835

Journal of the British Society of Master Glass-Painters 1980-81: Dr Hilary Wayment

Cotswold Life and Gloucestershire Life

New Scientist

Stroud Journal

The Telegraph Weekend: 2 March 2002, Mary Killen

The Times, 26 August 1819

Wilts and Gloucestershire Standard (various)

INDEX